Colorado

MAPPING THE CENTENNIAL STATE THROUGH HISTORY

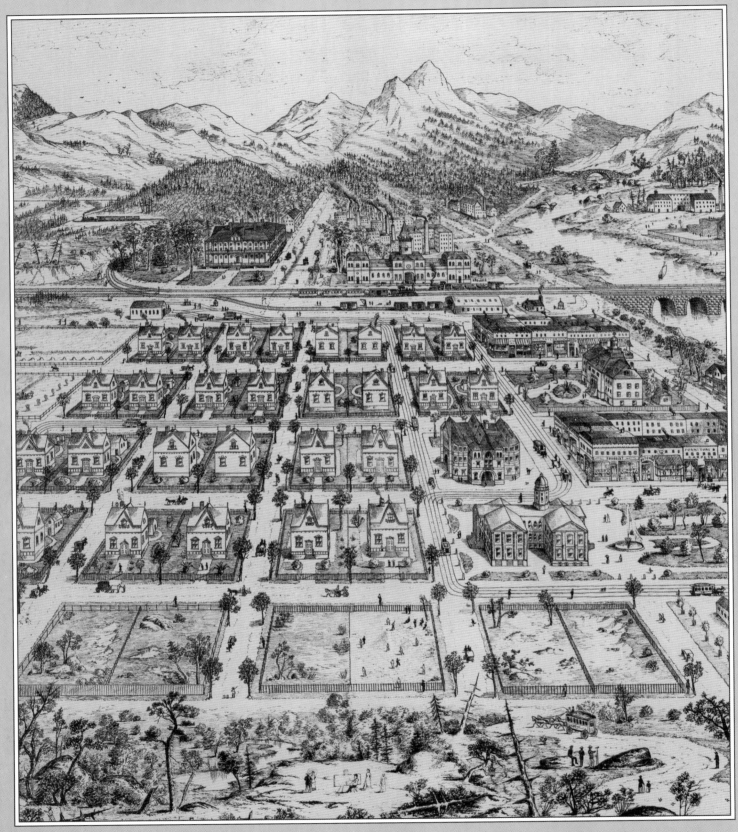

Detail of map on page 83

Colorado

MAPPING THE CENTENNIAL STATE THROUGH HISTORY

Rare and Unusual Maps from the Library of Congress

Vincent Virga

and Stephen Grace

Guilford, Connecticut

Text design: Sheryl P. Kober
Project editor: Julie Marsh

Library of Congress Cataloging-in-Publication Data.
Virga, Vincent.
  Colorado, a place in the American imagination : rare and unusual maps from the Library of Congress / Vincent Virga and Stephen Grace.
    p. cm.
  Includes bibliographical references.
  ISBN 978-0-7627-4531-9
  1. Colorado—History—Maps. 2. Colorado—Historical geography—Maps. 3. Early maps—Colorado—Facsimiles. 4. Colorado—Maps, Manuscript—Facsimiles. I. Grace, Stephen. II. Library of Congress. Geography and Map Division. III. Morris Book Publishing (Firm) IV. Title.

G1501.S1V5 2009
911'.788--dc22
                                    2009007029

Printed in China
10 9 8 7 6 5 4 3 2 1

Contents

Foreword

BY VINCENT VIRGA

ABOUT SEVENTY MILLION YEARS AGO, THE Rocky Mountains were rising out of the sea and southern Colorado was mostly a coastal swamp. As our historian Stephen Grace beautifully conjectures, comparatively little of the state is actually mountainous but the Rockies best define the state. They not only shape the landscape, they mirror the shape of Colorado's history. In his extraordinarily capable hands, the story is just as he describes it: ". . . one of lofty heights and sickening lows as dramatic as the topography of the Rockies, as thrilling as a descent down one of the state's unmarked ski runs plagued with jagged cliffs and blessed with blissful powder." And he and I both agree that maps can help us find our way not only through the mountains but through the past.

Living on planet Earth has always raised certain questions for those of us so inclined. Of course, the most obvious one is: Where am I? Well, as Virginia Woolf sagely noted in her diary, writing things down makes them more real; this may have been a motivating factor for the Old Stone Age artists who invented the language of signs on the walls of their caves in southern France and northern Spain between 37,000 and 11,000 years ago. Picasso reportedly said, "They've invented everything," which includes the very concept of an image.

A map is an image. It makes the world more real for us and uses signs to create an essential sense of place in our imagination. (One early example were the petroglyphic maps that were inscribed in the late Iron Age on boulders high in the Valcamonica region of northern Italy.) Cartographic imaginings not only locate us on this earth but also help us invent our personal and social identities since maps embody our social order. Like the movies, maps helped create our national identity—though cinema had a vastly wider audience—and this encyclopedic series of books aims to make manifest the changing social order that invented the United States, which is why it embraces all fifty states.

Each is a precious link in the chain of events that is the history of our "great experiment," the first and enduring federal government ingeniously deriving its just powers—as John Adams proposed—from the consent of

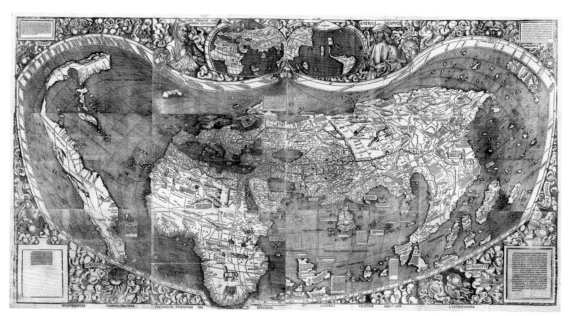
Waldseemüller map, 1507

am both a word person and a person who can think in pictures. This is the modus operandi of a map maker recording the world in images for the visually literate. For a traditional historian, maps are merely archival devices dealing with scientific accuracy. They cannot "see" a map as a first-person, visual narrative crammed with very particular insights to the process of social history. However, the true nature of maps as a key player in the history of the human imagination is a cornerstone of our series.

The very title of this volume, *Colorado: Mapping the Centennial State through History*, makes it clear that this series has a specific agenda, as does each map. It aims to thrust us all into a new intimacy with the American experience by detailing the creative process of our nation in motion through time and space via word *and* image. It grows from the relatively recent shift in consciousness about the physical, mental, and spiritual relevance of maps in our understanding of our lives on Earth. Just as each state is an integral part of the larger United States, "Where are we?" is a piece of the larger puzzle called "Who are we?"

The Library of Congress was founded in 1800 with 740 volumes and three maps. It has grown into the world's largest library and is known as "America's Memory." For me, its vast visual holdings made by those who helped build this nation make the Library the eyes of our nation as well. There are nearly five million maps in the Geography and Map Division. We have linked our series with that great collection in the hopes that its astonishing breadth will inspire us in our efforts to strike Lincoln's "mystic chords of memorys" and create living history.

On January 25, 1786, Thomas Jefferson wrote, "Our confederacy must be viewed as the nest from which all America, North and South is to be peopled." This is a man who could not live without books. This is a man who drew maps. This is a politician who in spite of his abhorrence of slavery and his respect for Native Americans took pragmatic rather than principled positions when confronted by both "issues." Nonetheless, his bold vision of an expanded American universe informs our current enterprise. There is no denying that the story of the United States has a dark side. What makes the American narrative unique is the ability we have displayed time and again to remedy our mistakes, to adjust to changing circumstances, to debate and then move on in new directions that seem better for all.

For Jefferson, whose library was the basis for the current Library of Congress after the British burned the first one during the War of 1812, and for his contemporaries, the doctrine of progress was a keystone of the Enlightenment. The maps in our books are reports on America, and all of their political programs are manifestations of progress. Our starting fresh, free of Old World hierarchies, class attitudes, and the errors of tradition, is wedded to our geographical isolation with its immunity from the endless internal European wars devastating humanity, which justify Jefferson's confessing, "I like the dreams of the future better than the history of the past." But, as the historian Michael Kammen explains, "For much of our history we have been present-minded; yet a usable past has been needed to give shape and substance to national identity." Historical maps keep the past warm with life and immediately around us. They encourage critical enquiry, curiosity, and qualms.

For me, this series of books celebrating each of our states is not about the delineation of property rights. It is a depiction of the pursuit of happiness, which is listed as one of our natural rights in the 1776 Declaration of Independence. (Thirteen years later when the French revolutionaries drafted a Declaration of the Rights of Man, they included "property rights" and Jefferson unsuccessfully urged them to substitute "pursuit of happiness" for "property.") Jefferson also believed, "The earth belongs always to the living generation." I believe these books depict what each succeeding generation in its pursuit of happiness accomplished on this portion of the earth known as the United States. If America is a matter of an idea, then maps are an image of that idea.

I also fervently believe these books will show the states linked in the same way Lincoln saw the statement that all men are created equal as "the electric cord in that Declaration that links the hearts of patriotic and liberty-loving men together, that will link those patriotic hearts as long as the love of freedom exists in the mind of men throughout the world."

VINCENT VIRGA
WASHINGTON, D.C.
INAUGURATION DAY, 2009

the governed. Each state has a physical presence that holds a unique place in any representation of our republic in maps. To see each one rise from the body of the continent conjures Tom Paine's excitement over the resourcefulness, the fecundity, the creative energy of our Enlightenment philosopher-founders: "We are brought at once to the point of seeing government begin, as if we had lived in the beginning of time." Just as the creators systemized not only laws but also rights in our constitution, so our maps show how their collective memory inspired the body politic to organize, codify, classify all of Nature to do their bidding with passionate preferences state by state. For they knew, as did Alexander Pope:

> All are but parts of one stupendous Whole
> Whose body Nature is, and
> God the soul.

And aided by the way maps under interrogation often evoke both time and space, we editors and historians have linked the reflective historical overviews of our nation's genesis to the seduction of place embedded in the art and science of cartography.

J. P. Harley posits, "The history of the map is inextricably linked to the rise of the nation-state in the modern world." The American bald eagle has been the U.S. emblem since 1782 after the Continental Congress appointed a committee in 1776 to devise an official seal for our country. The story of our own national geographical writing begins in the same period but has its roots centuries earlier, appropriately, in a flock of birds.

On October 9, 1492, after sailing westward for four weeks in an incomprehensibly vast and unknown sea during North America's migration month, an anxious Christopher Columbus spotted an unidentified flock of migrating birds flying south and signifying land—"Tierra! Tierra!" Changing course to align his ships with this overhead harbinger of salvation, he avoided being drawn into the northern-flowing Gulf Stream, which was waiting to be charted by Ben Franklin around the time our eagle became America as art. And so, on October 11, Columbus encountered the salubrious southern end of San Salvador. Instead of somewhere in the future New England, he came up the lee of the island's west coast to an easy and safe anchorage.

Lacking maps of the beachfront property before his eyes, he assumed himself in Asia because in his imagination there were only three parts to the known world: Europe, Asia, and Africa. To the day he died, Columbus doubted he had come upon a fourth part even though Europeans had already begun appropriating through the agency of maps what to them was a New World, a new continent. Perhaps the greatest visual statement of the general confusion that rocked the Old World as word spread of Columbus's interrupted journey to Asia is the Ruysch map of 1507. Here we see our nascent home inserted into the template created in the second century by Ptolemy, a

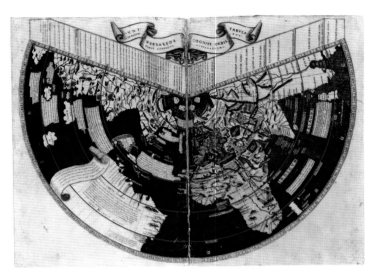

Ruysch map, 1507

mathematician, astrologer, and geographer of the Greco-Roman known world, the *oikoumene.*

This map changed my life. It opened my eyes to the power of a true cultural landscape. It taught me that I must always *look* at what I *see* on a map, focusing my attention on why the map was made, not who made it, when or where it was made, but *why.* The Ruysch map was made to circulate the current news. It is a quiet meditative moment in a very busy noisy time. It is life on the cusp of a new order. And the new order is what Henry Steele Commager christened the "utopian romance" that is America. No longer were maps merely mirrors of nature for me. No longer were the old ones "incorrect" and ignorant of the "truth." No longer did they exist simply to orient me in the practical world. The Ruysch map is reality circa 1507! It is a time machine. It makes the invisible past visible. Blessedly free of impos-

sible abstractions and idealized virtues, it is undeniably my sort of primary historical document.

The same year, 1507, the Waldseemüller map appeared. It is yet another reality and one very close to the one we hold dear. There we Americans are named for the first time. And there we sit, an independent continent with oceans on both sides of us, six years *before* Balboa supposedly discovered "the other sea." There are few maps as mysterious for cartographic scholars as Waldseemüller's masterpiece. Where did all that news come from? For our purposes it is sufficient to say to the world's visual imagination, "Welcome to us Americans in all our cartographic splendor!"

Throughout my academic life, maps were never offered to me as primary historical documents. When I became a picture editor, I learned to my amazement that most book editors are logocentric, or "word people." Along with most historians and academics, they make their livelihood working with words and ideas. The fact of my being an "author" makes me a word person, too, of course.

But I store information visually, as does a map. (If I ask myself where my keys are, I "see" them in my mind's eye; I don't inform myself of their whereabouts in words.) So I, like everyone who reveres maps as story-tellers,

Introduction

Before a young Wellesley College English professor named Katherine Lee Bates stood atop the 14,110-foot summit of Pikes Peak in 1893 and felt inspired to write the opening lines to "America the Beautiful," the land that today composes Colorado confounded and frustrated the area's earliest inhabitants. The great cliff dwellings of Mesa Verde were abandoned due at least in part to a prolonged and brutal drought. Intrepid explorers, rugged fur trappers and reckless prospectors were humbled, maimed, and killed amid mountains that today often seem to hold no more difficulty and danger than standing in a long lift line at a ski resort or experiencing an interruption in cellular service while fly-fishing. Whether viewed as a formidable obstacle to exploration and settlement or as a gorgeous backdrop for sightseeing and recreation, the Rockies have forever loomed large in the Colorado experience, and they have weaved a constant theme throughout the state's history.

Many first-time visitors to Colorado are surprised to learn that as majestic as Colorado's mountains are, comparatively little of the state is actually mountainous. Only slightly more than a third of Colorado's landmass is occupied by hills or mountains, and an even smaller percentage is actually home to the dramatic peaks for which the state is known. Nevertheless, Colorado's mean elevation of 6,800 feet makes it the highest state in the nation. The Rocky Mountains of Colorado boast fifty-four summits over 14,000 feet and one thousand peaks higher than 10,000 feet. From a dip in the landscape that measures 3,392 feet above sea level at the prairie town of Holly to the lofty summit of Mt. Elbert at 14,440 feet in the heart of Colorado's high country, the vertical relief of the state is staggering. Radiating like spokes from the hub of a wheel, Colorado's rivers leave their birthplace in the high peaks and flow in all directions toward the plains and valleys below. The great spine of the Rocky Mountains splits Colorado roughly down the middle along the Continental Divide, where waters part to the east and flow toward the

Detail of map on pages 74 and 75

Atlantic Ocean, and to the west, where they move toward the Pacific Ocean.

In the western end of the state, settled relatively late because it was cut off from all the human activity in the eastern end by the mountain barrier of the Rockies, stretch rugged plateaus and a challenging frontier of deserts, which are, somewhat paradoxically, blessed with swollen rivers.

Visitors to Colorado coming from the east, today as in times past, first encounter the flat, wide-open expanse of the Great Plains. From Colorado's eastern border the plains slope gently upward to the folded foothills of the Rocky Mountains and the stony peaks beyond. Plagued by dust storms, summer heat, scouring hail, and brutal winter blizzards, the eastern plains, with their rich, resilient grasses,

sustained vast herds of bison and the first Coloradans who hunted them; but the plains were considered by early Anglo-American explorers to be unfit for agriculture or human settlement. Eventually, from these arid prairies grew the main metropolitan areas of Colorado, in large part because of their proximity to the mountains, which held storehouses of precious minerals, most notably gold.

As the Spanish empire flourished in North America in the 1600s, legends of golden cities tucked into the mysterious mountains of a distant frontier inflamed the imaginations of Spanish adventurers. The area of present-day Colorado lay to the north of the land occupied by the Spanish and stretched into unknown wilderness beyond the boundary of their known world. To the earliest mapmakers, Colorado was yet to be named, much less charted, and simply appeared as blank spaces on maps with mountains sketched in north of the headwaters of the Rio Grande and a smattering of Spanish towns. The mountains of Colorado appeared as unnamed ranges running northward, like arrows pointing the imaginations of adventurers in search of gleaming treasure toward the unexplored frontier.

Spanish explorers never found gold in fabulous abundance amid the Colorado Rockies, and legends gave way to the reality of the mountains: soaring barriers of stone that impeded travel, weather whipped into deadly storms by peaks thrusting skyward, and oxygen-thin air filled with searing sun and deadly cold. The Colorado mountains nearly killed Lieutenant Zebulon Pike and his fellow explorers with heavy snow and frigid wind on the first American expedition sent to chart the region, and the blank places that Colorado would one day occupy on maps came to be viewed more with dread of the danger they harbored than with excitement for the potential riches they held.

This prevailing point of view changed suddenly in 1858, when on the plains at the base of the Rocky Mountains, in the place where Denver would grow, a discovery of gold was made. As fortune seekers rushed into the state, cartographers mapped the mountains as quickly as they could, filling in the blank spaces of the Rockies' convoluted topography.

At the same time they charted the progress of the trails and gold camps that arose seemingly overnight, first in the immediate vicinity of Denver and then throughout the state. As with the Spanish explorers before them, these early argonauts saw the mountains not as a barrier to human civilization but as a storehouse of wealth, a promised land of unimaginable bounty. Though some gold seekers did find the mother lode they lusted after and then retired to easy lives of luxury on the plains below, many mountain prospectors saw their dreams of easy riches give way to a reality as hard as the granite core of the Rockies. The frustrated prospectors struggled with altitude, wild weather, and terrain that seemed as hostile and alien as a moonscape. The maps of the goldfields that they clutched in their frostbitten fingers and viewed with eyes stinging from the sun and bitter wind began to look less like guides to troves of treasure and more like charts of some hellish region where humans were not meant to go.

The Colorado mountains claimed countless lives, and hundreds upon hundreds of towns collapsed into piles of ghostly rubble as they were abandoned when precious minerals played out. Railroaders blasted their way through the Colorado peaks, carving out tunnels, smoothing rough grades, and wrapping the mountains in endless miles of track. Next came the highway builders, surmounting the obstacles the mountains offered with their survey equipment and bulldozers, taming the renegade ranges with ribbons of pavement. Water engineers erected cement slabs of dams, carved out great basins for reservoirs, and laid a pipework of canals and conduits across the peaks, quieting the crashing flow of unruly rivers. Ski lifts were raised to whoosh recreation seekers to the tops of slopes.

Throughout this process of exploration and settlement, the Colorado land was used hard, and the mountains in particular paid a heavy price. Ancient forests fell to sawblades, fragile hillsides collapsed beneath bulldozers, pristine streams were poisoned by mining waste. Grasslands were grazed into oblivion, canyons disappeared beneath reservoirs. The bugling call of elk in autumn almost vanished from the wilderness, and for many years the silhouettes of eagles were seldom seen against the blue canopy of Colorado sky. Lynx were chased into the last pockets of primeval forest, the great bears that had terrified the first explorers fell to bullets and poisoned bait, and wolves disappeared into the steel jaws of spring-loaded traps. Citizens concerned about the fate of wildlife and wild landscapes in their state eventually steered public opinion away from a headlong rush to extract wealth from the land. They promoted a different approach, one that valued untrammeled wild places and aimed to preserve resources of clean water, healthy forests, and havens for animals so that future generations of Coloradans could partake of the state's natural wealth.

Perhaps Colorado's greatest value now lies in the relatively blank places on its maps: places where adventurous souls can still wander unfettered by the harsh lines of human roads and the strict geometry of town grids. Amid the Rocky Mountains, mapped boundaries give way to lore, and map legends are replaced by stories that bubble up from the deep recesses where our fears and dreams are born. In the state's wildest place, the Weminuche Wilderness, a person can disappear amid the immensity of a land unmarred by cartographic clues to human influence. And in the Weminuche, tales abound of grizzly bears that have survived the onslaught of civilization. These stories are perhaps rooted in actual observation, perhaps the product of myth. What is unquestionably true is that the Weminuche is wild and appears on contemporary maps as an enormous spread of land that is, if not perfectly blank as on the maps of old, at least unmarked by roads or any other human constructions. It is a half million acres in which the imagination can roam. It is a place for people harried by the pressures of civilization to dream up stories of giant trout in hidden alpine lakes. It is a place to hear the roar of a bear that is the remnant of a population that has, against all odds, survived the massive changes of the past centuries as the hunting and foraging of native people amid the mountains gave way to mines and roads and cars.

Now as in the past, there are still relatively empty places on the maps of Colorado's mountains, and within these raw expanses of land lie both blood-chilling terror and a beautiful bounty. In Colorado's ranges, heaving rivers capsize rafts, drowning thrill-seekers beneath their chilly waves, and avalanches bury modern-day adventurers, smothering their breath. But these wild places also hold riches so compelling they exert a magnetic pull on people from around the planet. The gold that put the Colorado mountains on the maps of pioneering cartographers has been replaced by the white gold of snow stashes that skiers eye on the lift maps printed by resorts. The copperplates of mapmakers have been relegated to museum displays; maps are now produced based on satellite imagery and computer programs so sophisticated they assemble virtual worlds from a jumble of numbers. The boundaries have been drawn, the blank places have been filled in. Yet there remain in the Colorado mountains, beyond the edges of marked ski runs, past the charted trails in the wilderness, the same deep reservoirs of mystery and lore that propelled the first adventurers into the empty spaces on the earliest maps of the frontier that would one day be called Colorado.

Colorado's history is filled with booms and busts. While there is far more to Colorado than mountains, those mountains best define the state, for the Rockies not only shape the landscape, they mirror the shape of Colorado's history. The story of Colorado is one of lofty heights and sickening lows as dramatic as the topography of the Rockies, as thrilling as a descent down one of the state's unmarked ski runs plagued with jagged cliffs and blessed with blissful powder. Colorado has made its share of mistakes: Episodes of senseless slaughter and illegal plunder stand alongside admirable tales of courage and determination. Colorado's history, like the wilderness it holds within its borders, may not always be pretty, but to navigate its intricate terrain, buckled and broken from the pressures of the shifting earth beneath it and raised toward airy heights, makes for a compelling journey. Maps can help us find our way, not only through the mountains but through the past.

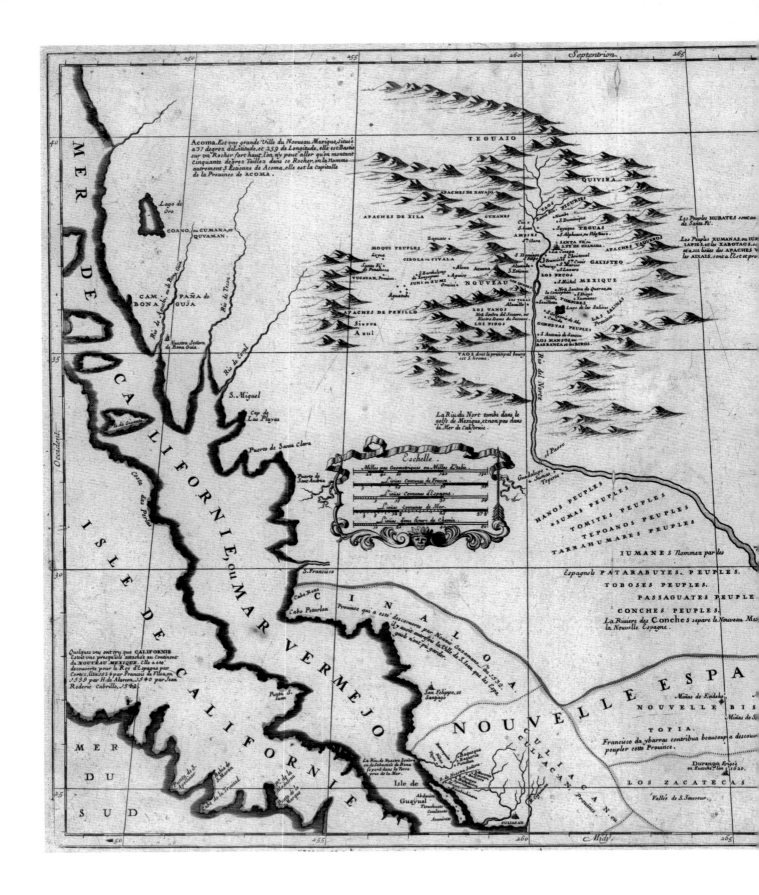

MER DE CALIFORNIE, ou MAR VERMEJO

ISLE DE CALIFORNIE

MER DU SUD

Occident

Septentrion

Midy

TEGUAIO

QUIVIRA

APACHES DE NAVAJO

APACHES DE XILA

MOQUI PEUPLES

CIBOLA ou CIVALA

APACHES DE PENILLO

Sierra Azul

NOUVEAU MEXIQUE

LOS TANOS

LOS PIROS

TAOS dont le principal bourg est S. Ierome

GORRETAS PEUPLES

LOS MANSOS, BARRANCA et les BIROS

Acoma. Est vne grande Ville du Nouveau Mexique, Situeé
a 37 degrez deLatitude, et 259 de Longitude, elle est Bastie
sur vn Rocher fort haut, l'on n'y peut aller qu'en montant
cinquante degrez Taillez dans ce Rocher, on la Nomme
autrement S. Estienne de Acoma, elle est la Capitalle
de la Prouince de ACOMA.

Lago de Oro

COANO, ou CUMANA, et QUVAMAN.

CAMPAÑA de BONA GUJA

Nuestra Señora de Bona Guia.

S. Miguel

Cap de Las Playas

Puerto de Santa Clara

Puerto de Sant Andrea

La Riu du Nort tombe dans le
golfe de Mexique, et non pas dans
la Mer de Californie.

Eschelle.
Milles pas Geometriques ou Milles D'Italie.
Lieües Communs de France.
Lieües Communs d'Espagne.
Lieües Communs de Mer.
Lieües d'une heure de Chemin.

Les Peuples HUBATES sont au de Santa Fe.

Los Peuples XUMANAS, ou TUMLAPIE, et les XABOTAOS, et a 112 lieües du APACHES les AIXAIS, sont a l'Est et pre

Guadalupe Sumas Topira

HANOS PEUPLES
SUMAS PEUPLES
TOMITES PEUPLES
TEPOANOS PEUPLES
TARRAHUMARES PEUPLES

IUMANES Nommez par les
Espagnols PATARABUYES, PEUPLES,
TOBOSES PEUPLES,
PASSAGUATES PEUPLE
CONCHES PEUPLES,
La Riuiere des Conches separe le Nouueau Me
la Nouuelle Espagne.

CINALOA

S. Francisco

Cabo Roxo

Cabo Peterlan

Prouince qui a esté descouuerte par Nunno Guzman, en 1532.
Il y auoit autrefois la Ville de S. Iean que les Espagnols n'ont pu garder.

San Felippo, et Sanpago

Punta S. Iuan

La Riu de Nuestra Señora
ou de Sebastian de Bona
se perd dans la Terre
pres de la Mar.

Isle de Guayual

CULIACAN

Quelques vns ont cru que CALIFORNIE
Estoit vne presqu'isle attachée au Continent
du NOUUEAU MEXIQUE. Elle a esté
decouuerte pour le Roy d'Espagne par
Cortez, l'an 1534 par Francois de Viloa en
1539 par H. de Alarcon, 1540 par Jean
Roderic Cabrillo, 1542.

NOUVELLE ESPA

NOUVELLE BIS

Miñas de Endehe

Miñas de S

TOPIA.

Francisco da ybarra contribua beaucoup a descou
peupler cette Prouince.

Durango Arges
en Rutsche l'an 1620.

LOS ZACATECAS

Vallee de S. Sauueur.

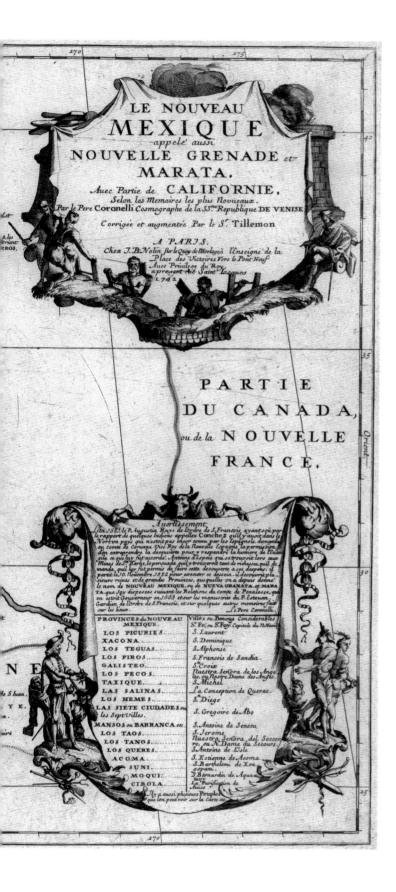

Le Nouveau Mexique appele aussi nouvelle grenade et Marata. Avec Partie de Californie (1688).

Esteemed Venetian cartographer Vincenzo Coronelli produced this map by copying information from a manuscript he found in Paris that had been created by Diego Penalosa, former governor and captain-general of New Spain, who was exiled and then settled in France. Because New Spain was an area little known to anyone other than the Spanish authorities, Penalosa's manuscript map was of the highest importance. After being exiled, Penalosa submitted several proposals to the French to attack New Spain; his manuscript was probably created in connection with one of these proposals. Penalosa's small sketch, which served as the basis for Coronelli's information about present-day Colorado on his celebrated map of the American West, focused on the Rio Grande, dividing it into two parts with two different names: the Río del Norte and the Río Bravo. Spanish towns are marked along the river, and vague mountain ranges cradle its headwaters and stretch north into the unexplored frontier of what would later become the state of Colorado. The exquisite craftsmanship of Coronelli's masterpiece, which was produced by engraving a copperplate and then making a strong, crisp impression on paper, marks the height of elegance in mapmaking.

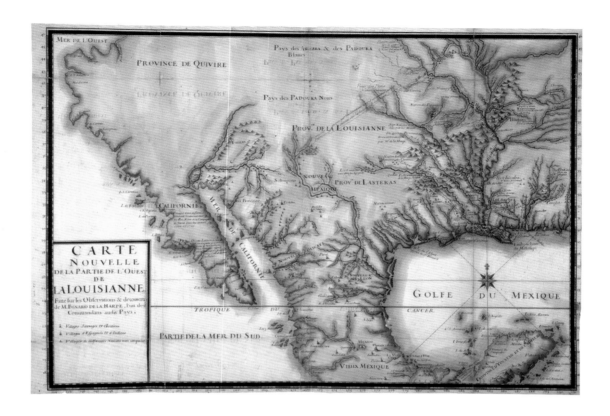

Carte Nouvelle de La Partie de L'Ouest de La Louisianne (1723–1725).

French explorer Bénard de La Harpe set off from New Orleans in 1719 to explore the plains between the Red and Arkansas Rivers and establish a French presence in this poorly understood area. Forming the boundary between the Louisiana frontier and the borderlands of New Spain, this area served as a constant point of friction between nations maneuvering for control of North American territory. Though La Harpe's manuscript map added to a geographic understanding of the lower Arkansas River, his explorations didn't take him upstream all the way into present-day Colorado. After gathering information from Wichita Indians about the upper reaches of the Arkansas, La Harpe guessed at its source and plotted it on his map, but the mountain highlands of Colorado that give birth to the river essentially remained a mystery to cartographers—a great unknown region awaiting exploration. Adding to the mystery was La Harpe's claim that he had found a unicorn on his travels. Furthermore, La Harpe's name is often associated with the legend of Emerald Rock, a fabulous jewel-encrusted stone hidden amid the Arkansas River wilderness. Though La Harpe denied that the search for this mythical treasure was one of the primary goals of his expedition, the legend persisted and left lingering rumors about great wealth in the unexplored reaches of Louisiana. Lieutenant Zebulon Pike would eventually probe this area by following the Arkansas River in 1806 into the mountain wilderness where it originates. One member of La Harpe's party, fore-shadowing the discovery that would eventually put Colorado on the map, wrote, "I have no doubt there are gold mines in the country, as we discovered a little stream which rolled gold dust in its waters."

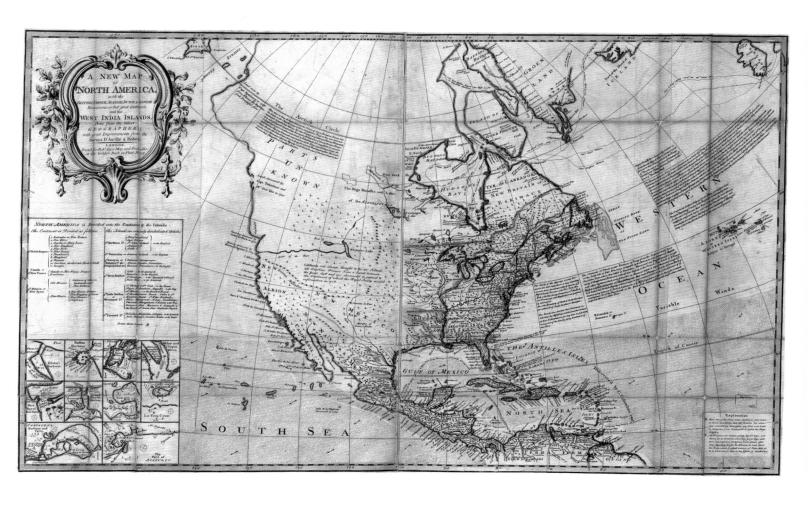

A new map of North America, with the British, French, Spanish, Dutch, and Danish dominions on that great continent; and the West India Islands, done from the latest geographers, with great improvements from the Sieurs d'Anville and Robert (1763).

This map published by Robert Sayer of London, England, makes clear that Colorado in 1763 was part of a stage for the geopolitical ambitions of European nations, but it provides little insight into the terrain of New Mexico and Louisiana that would later become Colorado. Colorado is essentially still a blank place with some randomly sketched mountains along the Rio Grande headwaters region north of Spanish settlements. The Spanish most likely knew much more about the northern regions of their New Mexico territory than appears here. Because they were very secretive about their discoveries, their accounts of exploration remained in manuscript form and were not published and thus generally didn't appear on maps produced by other countries.

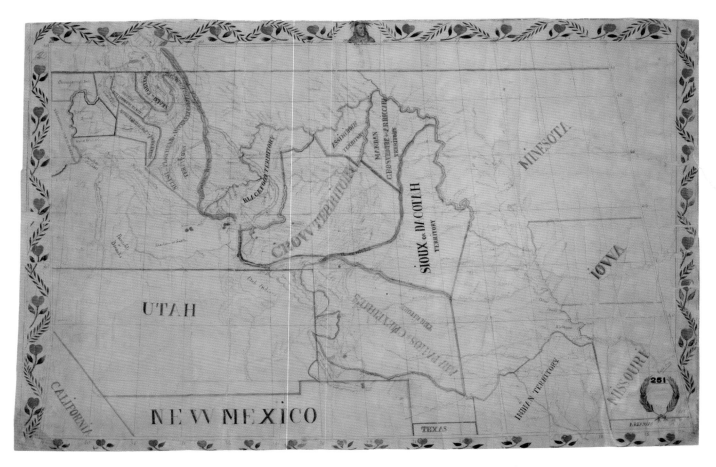

Map of the upper Great Plains and Rocky Mountains region respectfully presented to Col. D. D. Mitchell by P. J. de Smet (1851).

One of the great cartographic works of the American West, this manuscript map drawn by the Belgian Jesuit missionary Pierre-Jean de Smet was prepared to accompany the 1851 Treaty of Fort Laramie. Known by Native Americans as "Black Robe," de Smet was accepted by rival tribes and respected by them as a great religious leader who could mediate their disputes. He had extensive experience as a missionary to many tribes and was in contact with tribal chiefs, Indian agents, and frontiersmen such as legendary guide and trapper Jim Bridger. With the information he gathered, de Smet was able to create a detailed and accurate record both of physical geography and of the distribution of Plains Indian tribes in the area that would later become Colorado. The boundary lines delineating the tribes' territories were formalized by the U.S. government in the 1851 Treaty of Fort Laramie. These boundaries were in constant flux before the treaty, the result of Native Americans both migrating and being forcibly relocated by the U.S. government. The boundaries changed dramatically afterward as new treaties were forged following the realization that the land allocated to the Arapaho and Cheyenne was valuable to gold seekers and settlers. This map provides a static snapshot of a dynamic process that didn't reach a conclusion until more than a decade later, when the tribes of the eastern plains were removed from present-day Colorado.

Native People

LONG BEFORE CARTOGRAPHERS BEGAN TO FILL IN the blank places in the vast regions of the American West, the first Americans set foot in present-day Colorado. The earliest inhabitants of Colorado were Paleo-Indian hunters and nomadic gatherers who arrived in the area approximately fifteen thousand years ago after migrating overland from Asia across the Bering Strait land bridge and then dispersing southward through North America. They roamed across Colorado's eastern plains and western plateau, areas offering climate and terrain relatively mild in comparison to the jagged, storm-lashed heights of the Rocky Mountains. They moved in small groups, following herds of game and felling their prey of mammoths, sloths, and giant bison with stone-tipped spears. They set up temporary camps as they traveled and left scant traces to help future Coloradans understand their way of life.

Beginning around A.D. 600, the most complex culture in Colorado prior to European exploration developed in what is today the southwestern corner of the state. The Ancestral Puebloans, whom archaeologists previously referred to as Anasazi, made Mesa Verde their home for over seven hundred years, from A.D. 600 to A.D. 1300. They built multistoried structures of sandstone, mortar, and wood beams in the sheltered alcoves of deep canyon mazes. Their cities still stand as a tribute to their architectural skill, which reached its zenith during the Classic Period, beginning around 1100, when their civilization was composed of several thousand people. But for all their technological advancements, the Ancestral Puebloans were still vulnerable to Colorado's harsh landscape and shifting climate: An extended drought at the end of the thirteenth century dried up their lakes and killed their crops. They may also have strained their resources; after hundreds of years of intensive use, the land and its soils, forests, and animal populations may have been dangerously depleted, forcing them to leave their magnificent dwellings. Whatever the reason, after seven hundred years of thriving civilization in Colorado, the Ancestral Puebloans abandoned their cliff dwellings and migrated south to New Mexico and Arizona, where they became today's modern Pueblo people. They left behind at Mesa Verde pottery and baskets, roads and lookout towers, and entire cities made of stone. What they didn't leave behind was written words.

By the time the Spanish made the first European foray into Colorado in the mid-1500s, the Ancestral Puebloans had vanished. The Utes inhabited mountain valleys, and Apache, Comanche, and Kiowa tribes lived nomadic lives on the Great Plains, following herds of buffalo and deer to hunt, foraging for berries and roots, and living in tepees. The Spanish adventurers in Colorado, instead of laying waste to entire cultures as they had in the southern part of the future state, inadvertently helped the Colorado tribes strengthen control of their territory: The Spanish brought with them horses, which allowed the Native Americans of Colorado to travel farther and faster than they had before the Spanish arrived. The Utes became the first tribe to get horses, and they soon expanded their territory to include more than half of present-day Colorado. Tribes on the eastern plains also benefited from the horse, becoming more efficient hunters and warriors. Bands of Ute and Comanche riding Spanish horses sometimes descended from their strongholds in the north to raid the towns of New Mexico; the Spanish retaliated by sending troops

north into the mountains and plains of Colorado to punish the bellicose tribes.

Aside from introducing horses, Europeans changed the cultural landscape of the Native Americans in the area by pushing tribes in the eastern United States westward, forcing them into Colorado. Arapaho and Cheyenne moved on to the eastern prairies of Colorado as Anglo-Americans forged their way westward, shuffling the balance of power on Colorado's high plains. Warfare between the various groups of Native Americans in Colorado was continuous, but in the 1860s the tribes of the eastern plains stopped fighting among themselves and united against a new threat.

At first there was little friction between the white traders and trappers who trickled into Colorado and the Native Americans who occupied the land. The Arapaho, led by Chief Little Raven, welcomed the first pioneers who arrived on the banks of the South Platte River and Cherry Creek after gold was discovered. But as white settlers began pouring into the region in the ensuing gold rush, the great herds of bison disappeared, imperiling the way of life of the Native Americans, who depended on the animals to provide them with food, shelter, and clothing. Tension between the white settlers and the tribes of the eastern plains ratcheted up. In 1864 the conflict came to a head at Sand Creek, eighty miles southeast of Denver, when Civil War hero John Chivington led a regiment of Colorado Volunteers in a surprise attack on a Native American camp, whose occupants had been promised peace by the U.S. government. Chivington and his men slaughtered 163 Cheyenne and Arapaho people, mainly women, children, and the elderly, and they grotesquely mutilated the bodies of the slain and paraded them through the streets of Denver. At first celebrated as a great military victory, the massacre eventually drew widespread condemnation, but the fate of the Arapaho and Cheyenne in Colorado was sealed; they were soon removed from the eastern plains and relocated to the Wind River Indian Reservation in Wyoming.

As Anglo-Americans settled along the piedmont region at the edge of the Rockies and mined the central mountains, the Utes retreated to arid plateaus amid the wilderness of western Colorado. Though granted large reservations by the U.S. government, the Utes continually found whites encroaching on their land as fortune seekers spilled into the San Juan Mountains of southwestern Colorado in search of precious metals, and farmers, ranchers, and town builders spread across western Colorado in search of suitable land. Conflict between the two groups escalated, and in 1879 Nathan C. Meeker, the Indian agent at White River (near the present-day town of Meeker), and several employees were slain in a Ute uprising. Following the "Meeker Massacre," as the event came to be known, many Ute tribes were relocated to reservations in Utah, and Southern Utes were moved to reservations in what are now La Plata, Archuleta, and Montezuma Counties in southwestern Colorado. The land the Utes were expelled from was quickly occupied by white miners and settlers. Today, most of the state's Native American population is found on the Southern Ute Indian Reservation, the Ute Mountain Ute Indian Reservation, and in the Denver metropolitan area.

ELEVENTH CENSUS OF THE UNITED STATES:
ROBERT P. PORTER, SUPERINTENDENT.

INDIANS.

MAP OF
LINGUISTIC STOCKS
OF
AMERICAN INDIANS
chiefly within the present limits of the United States.
From Annual Report of Bureau of Ethnology Vol. 7.
by J. W. POWELL.

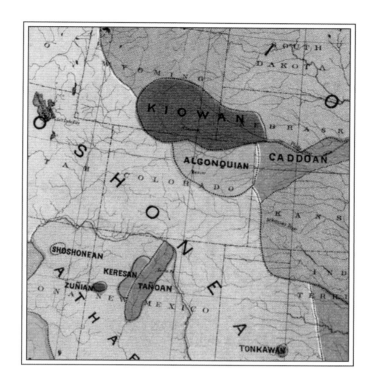

Map of linguistic stocks of American Indians (1890).

John Wesley Powell, aside from being a famed explorer and geologist who helped map the geography of the Western frontier, was an ethnologist and linguist who pioneered the serious study of Native American languages. This map demonstrates how cartography was one of the tools Anglo-Americans used in an effort to understand and document the differences between the many diverse tribes that played a prominent role in the American West. The Shoshonean, Algonquin, and Kiowan language groups are represented in Colorado, but the boundaries are somewhat arbitrary, both because the groupings were based on the superficial similarities of languages and because the Plains Tribes were constantly moving and the borders between them were forever morphing.

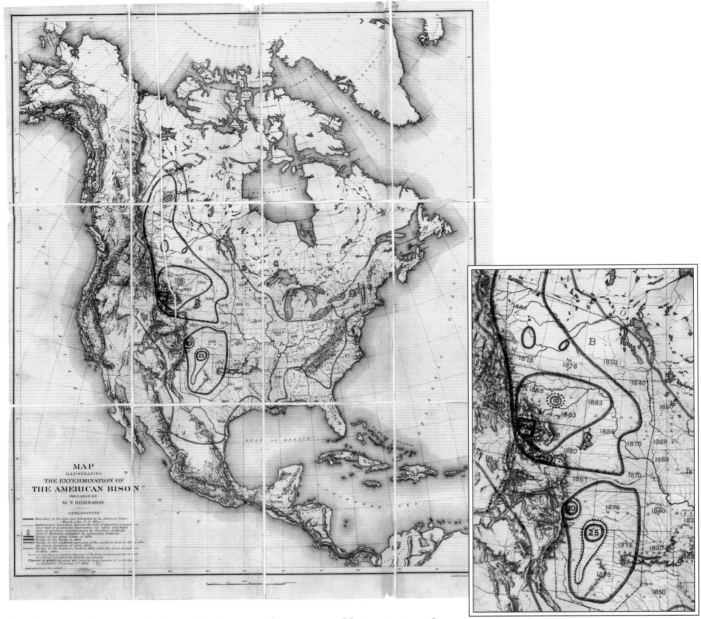

Map illustrating the extermination of the American bison, prepared by W. T. Hornaday;
compiled under the direction of Henry Gannett, E.M. (1889).

One of the most significant factors in the collapse of the cultures of Native Americans who inhabited the plains of eastern Colorado was the extermination of the bison, as documented in this map created by William Temple Hornaday. An early champion of American resource conservation, Hornaday dedicated himself to saving the species from extinction; he published this map as part of a detailed report titled *The Extermination of the American Bison*, which helped create public support to prevent the species from vanishing. Despite Hornaday's passionate efforts to preserve bison populations, their numbers dropped precipitously, and the tribes dependent upon them, such as the Arapaho and Cheyenne of the eastern Colorado plains, were devastated.

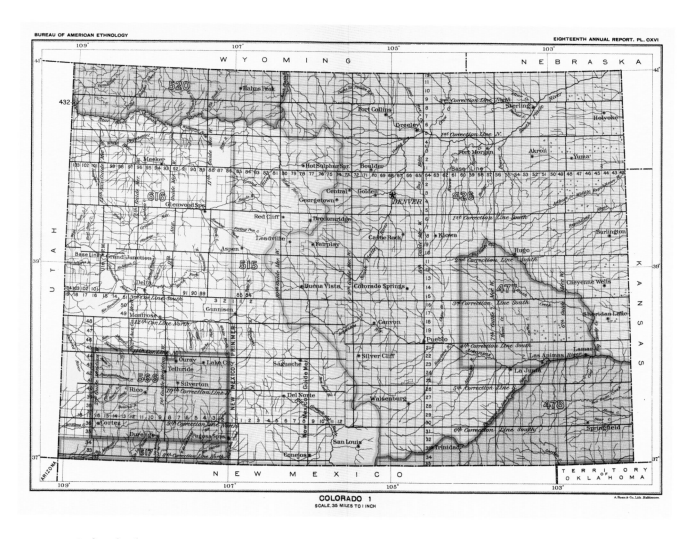

COLORADO 1

SCALE, 35 MILES TO 1 INCH

Indian land cessions in the United States, comp. by Charles C. Royce, with introduction by Cyrus Thomas—Colorado 1 (1896–1897).

As Colorado's native inhabitants surrendered the land that white prospectors and settlers were seeking, cartographic records of the dispossession were compiled. This map, published in the Eighteenth Annual Report of the Bureau of American Ethnology, displays numbered areas that correspond to a schedule of treaties and land cessions by which tribes gave up their territory.

18

Exploration

Three centuries after the Ancestral Puebloans abandoned their stone cities, another complex culture appeared in Colorado—that of the Spanish. The famed Spanish conquistador Francisco Vázquez de Coronado may have crossed the southeastern corner of Colorado on his return march to Mexico after a fruitless search for the Seven Cities of Cíbola. Coronado's foray northward into the shadowy borderland was propelled by legend. Around the year 1150 a myth originated in Spain when the Moors conquered Mérida. According to this legend, seven bishops fled the city to prevent the Muslim invaders from obtaining sacred religious relics and, after arriving in a mysterious, far-away land, founded seven cities that grew fabulously wealthy due to an abundance of gold. This legend remained with Spanish adventurers through the centuries and followed them to the New World, where expeditions, including that of Coronado in 1540, set off into the mountainous frontier to the north of New Mexico in search of mythical cities made of gold.

Beginning in the mid-1600s, from their strongholds to the south, the Spanish made periodic forays northward, claiming all of what is now Colorado for the Spanish crown. In 1765 Don Juan Maria de Rivera, following rumors of bountiful wealth hidden amid the mountains of the north, led a Spanish expedition into the San Juan and Sangre de Cristo Mountains in search of gold and silver. The expedition returned not with riches but with new knowledge of the Colorado wilderness.

Derrotero hecho por Antonia Vélez y Escalante, misionero para mejor conocimiento de las misiones, pueblos de indios y presidios que se hallan en el Camino de Monterrey a Santa Fe de Nuebo Mexico (1777). Produced by Bernardo Miera y Pacheco, an esteemed surveyor and mapmaker who was part of the Dominguez-Escalante Expedition, this is considered the first surviving manuscript map of Colorado. The expedition described important geographic details about the previously unexplored expanse of western Colorado, characterizing the Rocky Mountains as "the spine of North America" and noting the ancient cliff dwellings of Mesa Verde.

Aside from the official expeditions launched by the Spanish, there were Spanish forays into Colorado of a furtive nature. Spanish prospectors sneaked northward from New Mexico into the borderland, quietly probing the mountains in search of gold and silver. Because by law they had to pay the Spanish king one-fifth of all the riches they found, they made no announcements of gold strikes and left behind no written accounts of their adventures, giving rise to rumors of secret Spanish gold mines hidden in the Rockies. Adventurous Coloradans to this day scour maps and trek through the hills in search of clues to lost Spanish mines and their storied golden riches.

In July of 1776 Franciscan priests Francisco Atanasio Domínguez and Silvestre Vélez de Escalante set out from Santa Fe, seeking an overland route to the California missions. But after failing to reach Spanish settlements along the Pacific Coast, they returned to Santa Fe in January of 1777. Though they didn't reach California, their expedition traveled far into the unknown central Rockies, traversing what is now western Colorado as far north as the White River in Rio Blanco County. A member of the expedition produced the first surviving map of Colorado. The map was not published, but multiple manuscript copies were created and circulated throughout New Spain.

The Spanish never discovered the fabled treasure they sought in Colorado. They didn't forge the trail they hoped would link the dis-parate parts of their New World empire, nor did they settle their northern border beyond Santa Fe. But their travels across the uncharted wilds of what would one day be called Colorado aided future explorers and left a legacy of evocative place names: mountain ranges called Sangre de Cristo ("Blood of Christ") and Sierra de las Grullas ("Mountains of the Cranes"); rivers named La Plata ("silver") and Animas (originally named by the Spanish "Rio de las Animas Perdidas," meaning "River of the Lost Souls"); and the name Colorado itself ("colored red").

In 1800 Spain ceded a vast area, including most of present-day eastern Colorado, to Napoleon Bonaparte and the French. Three years later this enormous parcel of land was sold by Napoleon to the United States in the Louisiana Purchase, and a new nation hungry for growth and expansion set out to explore the frontier it had acquired. In 1806, as the Lewis and Clark Expedition was heading homeward, an expedition led by Lieutenant Zebulon Pike embarked to map the southern part of the Louisiana Purchase.

Among the goals of the expedition were to explore and map the headwaters of the Arkansas River and then to proceed south to locate the source of the Red River and follow it to the Mississippi. This region formed an amorphous buffer between the land acquired in the Louisiana Purchase and Spanish territory; the border separating the colliding empires was not clearly defined because the geography of the Arkansas and Red Rivers had yet to be thoroughly explored and accurately mapped. As with the Lewis and Clark expedition, Pike's group was instructed to study and catalogue natural resources and subjects of scientific interest and to gather information about the Native American inhabitants of the region.

Along with the official orders, Pike was also issued a set of secret orders by General James Wilkinson. At the time the highest-ranking officer in the U.S. Army, Wilkinson commissioned Pike to lead the expedition to the Spanish borderlands without the authorization of President Thomas Jefferson or the War Department. Wilkinson may have been a Spanish spy, but historians aren't certain what he was up to, and his exact intentions remain a mystery. It is possible that, in cahoots with U.S. vice president Aaron Burr, he was planning a coup in the West—either as a traitorous act to separate the western territories from the Union or as a patriotic plot to conquer Spanish territory without officially involving the U.S. government. Historians generally agree that Pike was unaware of the Wilkinson-Burr plot and knew only that his mission was to gather as much intelligence about the Spanish as possible for the United States.

Pike and fifteen other men started up the Arkansas in late October, following the trail of a troop of Spanish cavalry. Despite not having the clothing, equipment, and supplies necessary for winter travel and being warned by Native Americans who had contact with the Spanish that his party should turn back, Pike pressed on and reached the site of modern-day Pueblo in November 1806. Mesmerized by a peak that he thought resembled a "small blue cloud" as he approached the Rockies, Pike set off with a few men to climb the mountain. Several days later, after severely underestimating the distance involved because he was unused to the clear, dry air, and after being impeded by waist-deep snow before reaching the summit, Pike returned with his climbing party to camp and proclaimed the mountain impossible to climb. On the map of his journey that he produced, Pike labeled the mountain simply as "Highest Peak," and in his journal he recorded its elevation as more than 18,000 feet.

Pike next led his expedition up the north fork of the Arkansas, then left the river and wandered overland, eventually becoming lost. At one point he thought he had located the Red River, but Pike's expedition was actually back on the Arkansas, seventy miles upstream from where they had left it a couple of weeks earlier. As blizzards raged, the temperature plummeted and snow on the ground deepened. The desperate group worked its way back downriver, the ice of the Arkansas thick enough to support their horses, the huge vertical walls of the Royal Gorge rising above them. With his group battling frostbite, gangrene, and starvation, Pike, still determined to locate the Red River, left a few men behind and headed southward. He crossed the San-gre de Cristo Mountains, eventually reaching the site of present-day Great Sand Dunes National Park and the headwaters of the Rio Grande, which Pike, once again, wrongly concluded was the Red River. Deep in Span-ish territory, he built a small stockade near present-day Alamosa, above which he flew the U.S. flag. Pike, who had been instructed by Wilkinson to scout as closely as possible to Santa Fe and if captured by the Spanish to feign being lost, had indeed, most scholars believe, actually become quite lost.

Spanish soldiers, upon discovering Pike and then rounding up the rest of his bedrag-gled party, who were scattered across the mountains, marched them down to Santa Fe. After being questioned and having his note-books confiscated, Pike was sent by Spanish authorities back home in order to avoid caus-ing a conflict with the United States. However bungled Pike's expedition may have been, it did provide valuable cartographic clues to the Arkansas River region of the Spanish border-lands, and it produced the first detailed maps of eastern Colorado. Pike managed to smug-gle notes in the barrels of the rifles he was allowed to take with him when he returned to America. From those notes he reconstructed a map, the first to accurately chart the Arkansas and its tributaries. Much of the information on his map, however, was borrowed by Pike from the cartography of noted German geog-rapher Alexander von Humboldt, who visited

Mexico City and was given access to Span-ish archives. Pike did not credit Humboldt, and so Pike, who explored the Arkansas River region, plagiarized the map of Humboldt, who had never been there, producing one of the American West's most iconic maps.

In 1820 Major Stephen Long was sent by President James Monroe to explore the southwestern boundary of the Louisiana Pur-chase and to produce a scientific inventory of its contents. His party traveled up the South Platte River, passing the sites of present-day Greeley, Denver, and Colorado Springs. They spotted what was later named Longs Peak, and they traveled toward the mountain that Pike had identified as the highest and most formidable of the Rocky Mountains. The expedition's botanist, Dr. Edwin James, docu-mented alpine wildflowers in riotous bloom on the mountain's slopes, and with some other members of the party, he managed to scale its summit, defying Pike's prediction that no human would ever set foot on its highest point. Long named the mountain James Peak, but trappers and traders insisted on calling it Pikes Peak. The latter name stuck, and the brave botanist was all but forgotten, save for a lesser peak farther north named for him.

Long produced a map of the region in which he identified the eastern plains along the Rocky Mountain Front Range, where Colorado's main metropolitan cor-ridor would eventually grow, as part of the "Great American Desert." In the report that accompanied the map, Long stated that the area was "almost wholly unfit for cultivation and, of course, uninhabitable by a people depending upon agriculture for their subsistence." Long concluded that the region was best left as a wilderness wasteland to serve as a buffer against the Spanish, British, and Russians, who at the time shared the continent with the Americans and were all vying for control of its land and resources. Looking at the great metropolitan sprawl along the Colorado Front Range today, Long's assertion might seem absurd, but given the technology of the 1820s, his belief that the eastern plains of Colorado would never be settled doesn't seem unreasonable. Timber for houses and fuel was scarce, as was surface water. Hard, sandy soil and harsh winters made life on the prairie seem precarious at best, even though bison blackened the plains in their multitudes and Native Americans had been living there for centuries.

Following the lead of explorers such as Pike and Long, more expeditions penetrated the uncharted expanses of Colorado and gradually began filling in the blank places on maps of the Rocky Mountain West. Beginning in the 1820s American trappers started venturing into what is now Colorado, gathering beaver pelts from mountain streams and buffalo hides from the plains and selling them at trading posts that quickly emerged to serve the burgeoning fur industry. Bent's Fort, located on the Arkansas River along the Santa Fe Trail, one of the primary routes of travel through the area for early explorers and mountain men, grew to be the most important of the High Plains trading hubs. It was a bustling center of activity amid the Colorado wilderness where Americans, Mexicans, and Indians swapped goods and traded cultures in a period of relative peace.

But war lay on the horizon. The Republic of Texas declared its independence from Mexico in 1836, and the breakaway republic's southern and western boundary with Mexico along the Rio Grande in what is now Colorado was under constant dispute. After the United States annexed the Republic of Texas in 1845, this border conflict served as one of the triggers for the Mexican-American War. In 1846, when war broke out between Mexico and the United States, General Stephen Kearny marched troops along the Santa Fe Trail and used Bent's Fort as a staging area before entering Mexico. After being quickly trounced by American troops, Mexico, by the Treaty of Guadalupe Hidalgo in 1848, ceded to the United States most of what was to become Colorado that had not already been acquired in the Louisiana Purchase.

Though large in area and boasting a wealth of resources, this region that would later be admitted to the Union as the state of Colorado was still a wild frontier that offered little of interest to Anglo-Americans other than the hardiest explorers, trappers, and traders. But this would soon change.

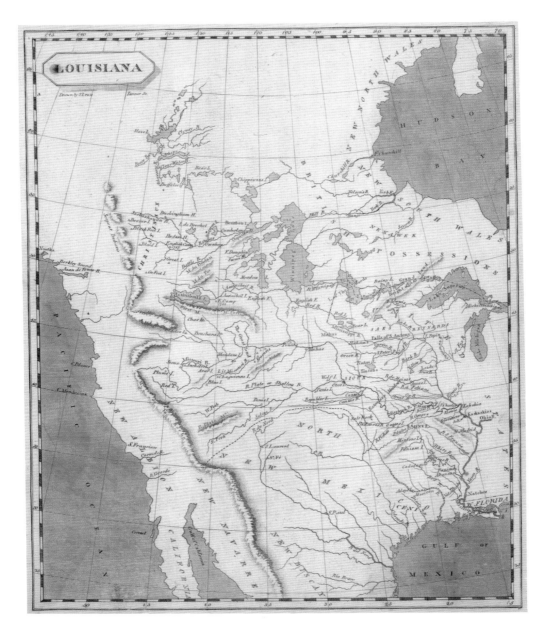

Louisiana. From Arrowsmith & Lewis New and Elegant General Atlas (1804).

This map makes clear how little was known about the area of what is now Colorado at the time of the Louisiana Purchase. The scale of the American West and the distances and difficulties involved in traveling through it and settling it were not understood at this point. Features such as the Rocky Mountains, which are depicted here as a single range close to the West Coast, are more the product of guesswork and wishful thinking than of scientific surveying. Guiding early attempts to map Louisiana were false cartographic assumptions, such as the "pyramidal height-of-land" theory, which postulated that America's great rivers all originated from one mythical central high point in the mountains of the West, and "symmetrical geography," which claimed that western mountains were mirror images of ranges in the East such as the Blue Ridge and Appalachian. Mapmakers began the long process of accurately filling in details as explorers set out to survey the vast wilderness purchased from France.

A Chart of the Internal Part of Louisiana (1810).

Zebulon Pike produced this map after his famous reconnaissance of the West and his capture by Spanish troops. Pike was the first writer in English to describe landmarks now familiar on Colorado maps, such as South Park, the Royal Gorge, and the mountain that bears his name. Though much of the map is accurate, the erroneous pyramidal-height-of-land theory—the baseless belief in a central high point of land from which major rivers spill—was alive and well on Pike's map: the land surrounding what he labels "Highest Peak" (later named Pikes Peak in his honor) is a place in the mountains born both of observation and creative guesswork that fancifully forms the common source of several western rivers. Published before maps of Lewis and Clark's epic journey were officially released, Pike's map and the account of his adventures in the Spanish borderlands captivated the imagination of the American public.

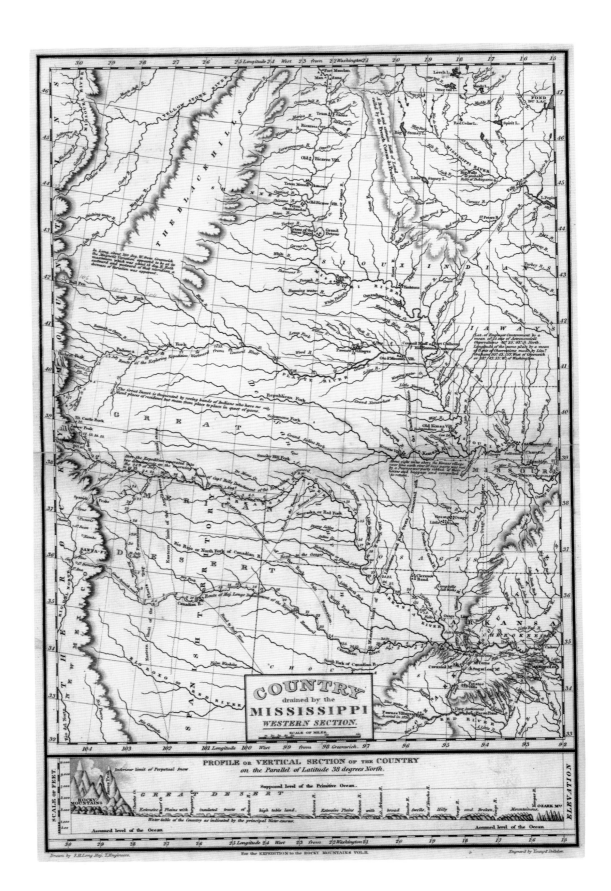

Country drained by the Mississippi, drawn by S.H. Long (1823).

A scientific expedition headed by Major Stephen H. Long to record plant and animal life and geological formations led him along the South Platte River through present-day Colorado and resulted in this map, which corrected many geographical errors made by previous expeditions and which famously labeled the eastern plains of Colorado part of the "Great American Desert." Long believed this region was a brutal wasteland unfit for human habitation and would never be settled. Millions of Denverites and denizens of other Front Range cities located in Long's Great American Desert would tend to disagree.

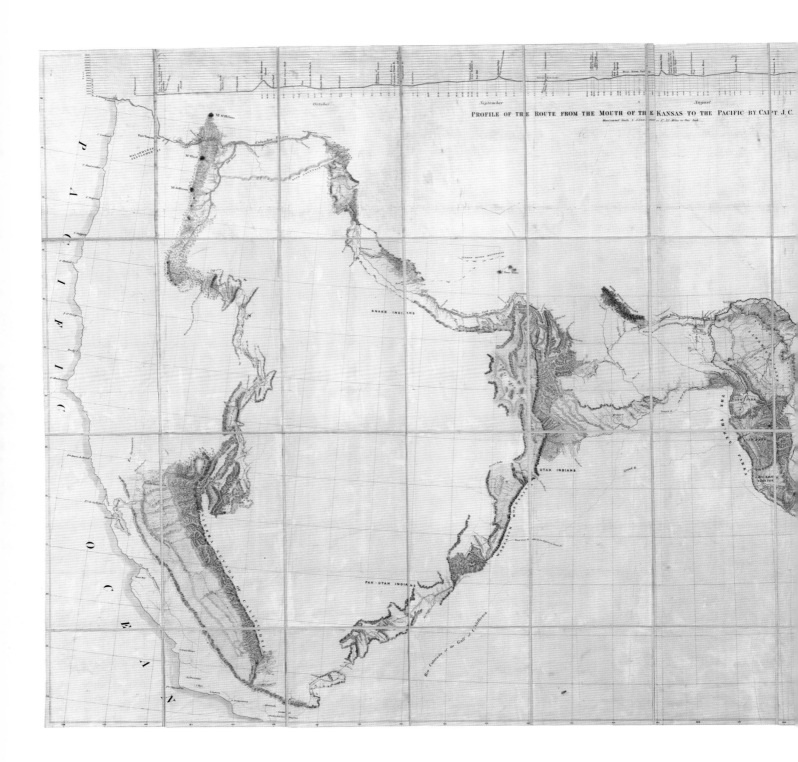

October

September

August

PACIFIC

OCEAN

SIERRA NEVADA OF CALIFORNIA

SNAKE INDIANS

UTAH INDIANS

PAH-UTAH INDIANS

Rio Colorado of the Gulf of California

THE THREE PARKS

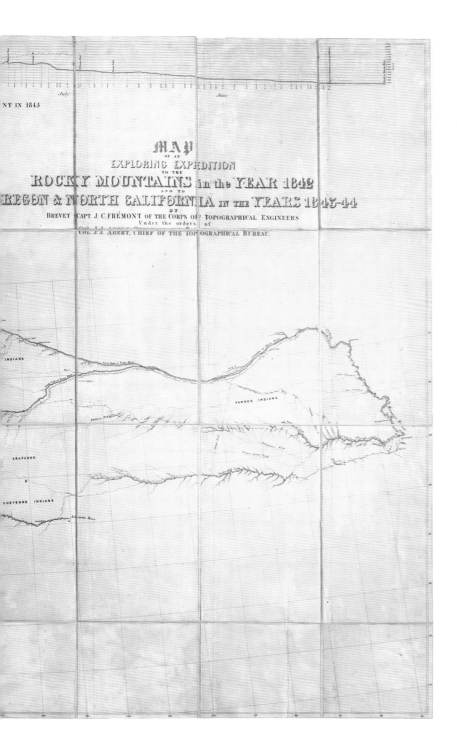

Map of an exploring expedition to the Rocky Mountains in the year 1842 and to Oregon & north California in the years 1843–44, by Brevet Capt. J. C. Frémont of the Corps of Topographical Engineers under the orders of Col. J. J. Abert, Chief of the Topographical Bureau.

Lieutenant John C. Frémont, dubbed "The Great Pathfinder," made five major expeditions in the West, each of which passed through Colorado. Frémont, a relentless self-promoter, hired legendary frontier scout and soldier Kit Carson to guide him. He also employed one of the most skilled surveyors and mapmakers of the time, George Karl Ludwig (Charles) Preuss. German by birth and famously melancholy by temperament, Preuss's careful observations made clear the vast distances and tremendous difficulties inherent in traversing the central Colorado Rockies and resulted in maps such as this one, which helped guide future explorers. There are large blank spaces on this map because Preuss recorded only what he surveyed based on scientific measurements of latitude and longitude; he did not rely on secondhand accounts or conjecture in his precise cartography. "The Three Parks," high mountain valleys tucked behind the Front Range, were features of Colorado's terrain long known to trappers, but they were documented for the first time in a published map by Frémont's expedition.

Mapa de los Estados Unidos de Méjico: segun lo organizado y definido por las varias actas del congreso de dicha république y construido por las mejores autoridades (1847).

Though much of the information on this map created by an American cartographer in New York was plagiarized and geographically inaccurate, it guided the treaty that led to one of the largest land transfers in American history. Published on the eve of the war with Mexico, it was used for the negotiations that preceded the Treaty of Guadalupe Hidalgo, in which the United States acquired much of the land that would later become Colorado. The map depicts a long, skinny stretch of territory ("a stovepipe") extending north to the forty-second parallel that was claimed by the Republic of Texas. The U.S. government purchased this claim from Texas, and along with the territory taken from Mexico, the stovepipe eventually became part of what is Colorado today. The craftsmanship used to produce this map is significant; it is a fine example of copperplate engraving and hand coloring, techniques that were soon to be superseded by lithography and production methods cheaper and less time consuming—but also less visually pleasing.

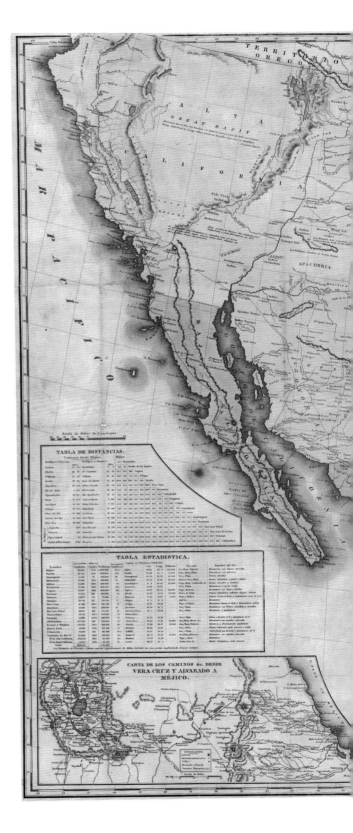

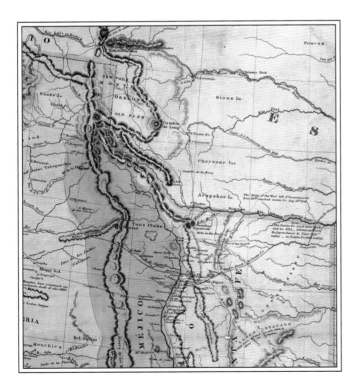

MAPA
de los
ESTADOS UNIDOS
DE
MÉJICO,

*Segun lo organizado y definido por las varias
actas del Congreso de dicha República, y
construido por las mejores autoridades.*

LO PUBLICAN J. DISTURNELL, 102 BROADWAY.
(NUEVA YORK.)
1847.

Scale of English Miles. REVISED EDITION.

31

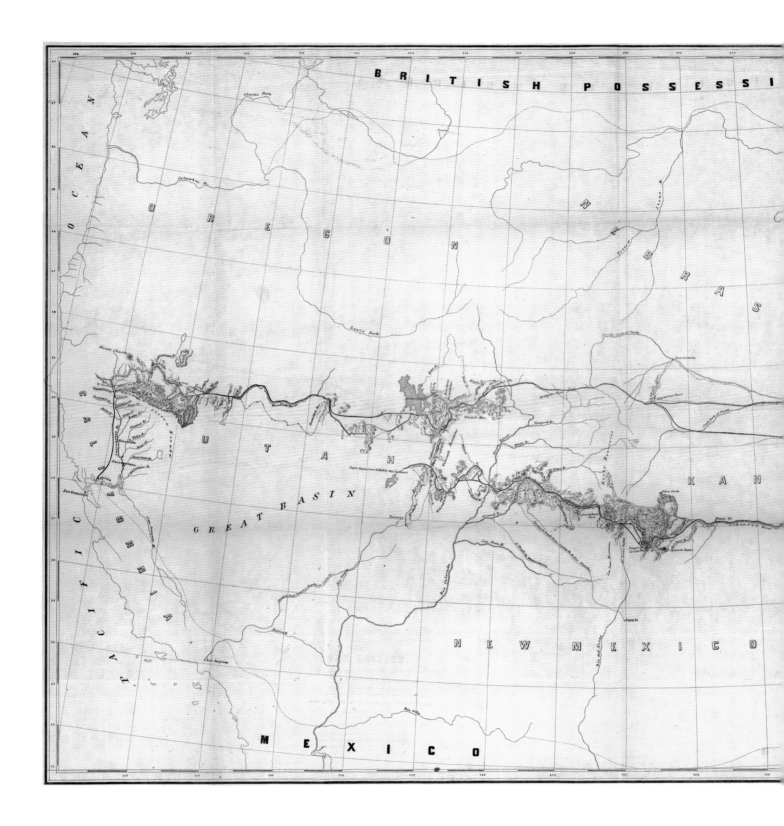

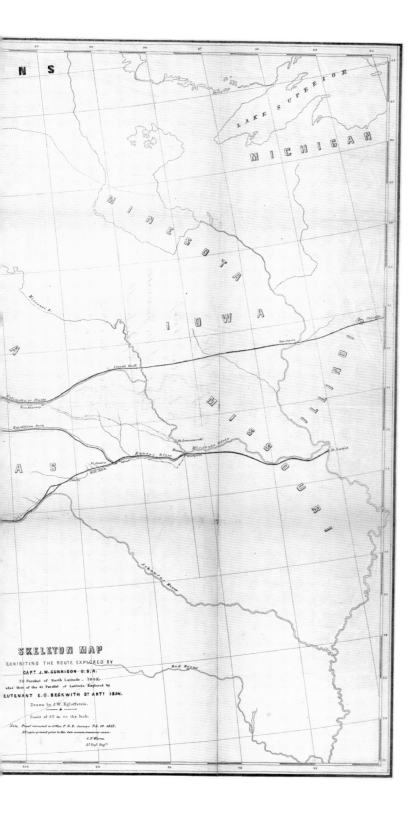

Skeleton map exhibiting the route explored by Capt. J. W. Gunnison U.S.A., 38 parallel of north latitude (1853), also that of the 41 parallel of latitude explored by Lieutenant E.G.P. Beckwith 3d. Arty. (1854).

Captain John W. Gunnison led an exploratory party to survey a route for a transcontinental railroad between the thirty-eighth and thirty-ninth parallels. He passed through the Tomichi Valley, where the town of Gunnison is named in his honor, and then he encountered the imposing Black Canyon, carved by the Gunnison River, also named in his honor. A county and a national forest in Colorado also bear his name. This is a "path map": Gunnison's expedition wasn't sent to explore wilderness for the sake of exploration or to perform scientific surveys of the land; they had the very specific task of charting a railroad route. Gunnison was murdered by a band of Utes rumored to have been acting on behalf of a secret Mormon militia under the direction of Mormon leader Brigham Young, who was concerned that a railway would cause an influx of non-Mormon settlers to the Utah Territory. But Gunnison's expedition was a success: It was the first to chart a transcontinental railroad route through Colorado's central Rocky Mountains.

General geological map of Colorado Department of the Interior,
U.S. Geological and Geographical Survey of the Territories;
F. V. Hayden, U.S. geologist in charge (1877).

In the late nineteenth century distinguished geologist Dr. Ferdi-
nand Vandeveer Hayden led several pioneering survey expeditions
of the Rocky Mountains. Hayden's systematic exploration resulted
in a detailed study of Colorado and an accurate atlas of the state.
His work became the basis for all subsequent mapping projects in
Colorado.

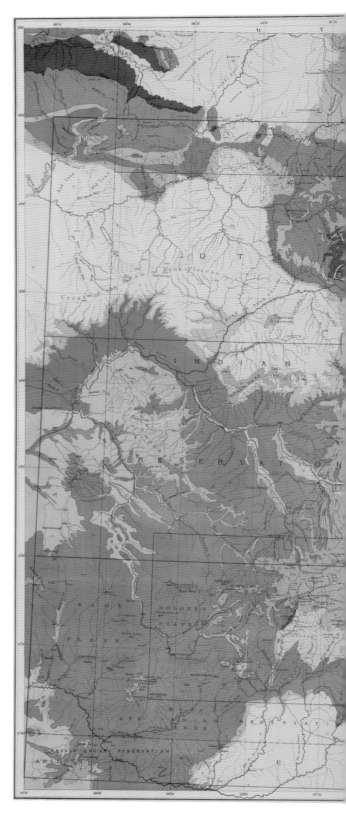

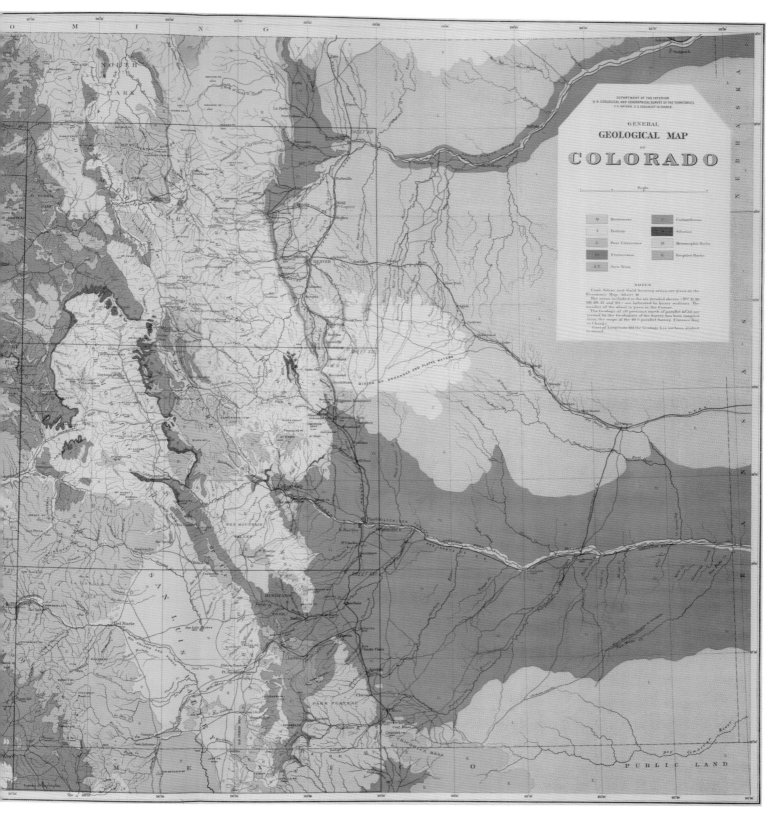

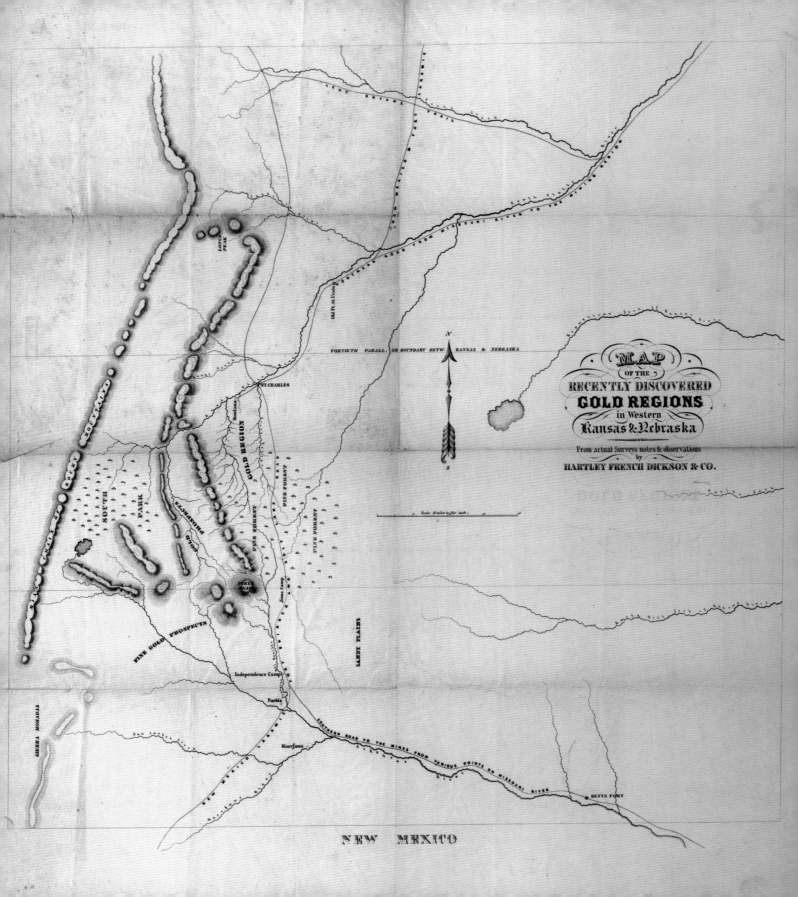

Pikes Peak Gold Rush

THE MOST EVENTFUL PERIOD IN COLORADO'S history began with rumors. Tales of goldfields in the Colorado mountains piqued the interest of Easterners suffering from a financial panic that left hordes of people desperately poor and dreaming of ways to restore their wealth. While Americans mulled over their dismal business options in 1858, the forty-niners who had headed west during the California Gold Rush reminisced about the gleaming dust they had panned from Rocky Mountain rivers when pausing on their way to California. A Delaware Indian told stories of shiny nuggets he'd seen strewn across the bed of a stream that rushed out of the mountains and onto the High Plains. Colorado had not yet been named, and its land, consisting of Louisiana Purchase and Mexican War acquisitions, was still wild. It appeared on maps as a place with vague boundaries, part of a sprawling western frontier slowly filling in, with mountain ranges mapped by explorers and trails blazed by trappers and traders. Between these known landmarks lay stretches of rough, unmapped country, and upon these ill-defined recesses of mountain wilderness, Americans could project their dreams. In 1858, when men and women with rich imaginations huddled around maps of the western frontier and studied the empty places yet to be charted, they didn't see hardship and danger. They saw the solution to all their problems. They saw the fulfillment of all their fantasies. They saw gold.

In the spring of 1858, an expedition comprising mining veterans from the goldfields of Georgia and California followed reports of gold to Ralston Creek, near present-day Denver. Discouraged after a few days of unsuccessful

Map of the recently discovered gold regions in Western Kansas & Nebraska, from actual surveys notes, & observations by Hartley French Dickson & Co. (1859).

This is the first map to depict the Front Range of Colorado and to document the Pikes Peak Gold Rush. In the spring of 1858, William Hartley, a civil engineer and surveyor, joined a party that traveled west to prospect for gold. In September they laid out a townsite at the confluence of the South Platte River and Cherry Creek and called it St. Charles. As Hartley's group left to follow the South Platte River back east, the Larimer Party jumped the townsite and renamed it Denver City. This map shows St. Charles as the main settlement in the area. Later maps referred to it as Denver, and St. Charles vanished from maps and from memory. Hartley never returned. From the East he published a guidebook with a map to the new goldfields and tables showing camping places and distances along the routes. It was among the first of many guidebooks written for the "fifty-niners" who flooded what is today Colorado in search of gold.

searching, most of these prospectors returned home. The persistent few who stayed behind discovered in July of 1858 a few hundred dollars' worth of surface gold in Cherry Creek, a tributary of the South Platte River. Though the gold strike was insignificantly small, a trader got wind of the discovery and took some gold samples back east with him, telling everyone he met along the way about the find. General William Larimer, following word of the discovery, led a group of men to Cherry Creek, where Larimer's group established a settlement after illegally jumping another town claim made by men who'd arrived before them. Larimer named his new town Denver City in honor of James W. Denver, governor of the Kansas Territory, in which the settlement that would grow into the city of Denver was situated. Thus Denver, founded in a criminal act and comprising no more than a stake in the ground and a couple of ramshackle cabins, came into being.

Newspaper headlines such as "THE NEW ELDORADO!!! GOLD IN KANSAS TERRITORY" trumpeted exciting news across a nation reeling from financial calamity and desperate with dreams of easy riches. Pikes Peak, though located south of Denver and not near the gold discovery, was easy to see from the plains and became an emblematic landmark for pioneers in search of rich deposits. By the spring of 1859, prospectors with PIKES PEAK OR BUST! written on their wagons were racing across the parched and sprawling wilds of the

Great American Desert toward Denver. Some poor souls in the grip of gold fever came on foot, pushing all their worldly belongings in wheelbarrows.

As this westward migration became a veritable flood, newspaper editors in the East began asking why no gold was being sent back from the new El Dorado. But just as newspapers started running stories about the "Great Bamboozle" and hordes of disgruntled gold seekers began turning back, big strikes were made by persistent prospectors who ventured into the mountains. A gold discovery forty miles west of Denver led to the establishment of the twin towns of Central City and Black Hawk. To govern these unruly gold camps plagued by the chaos of jumped mining claims and general lawlessness, pioneers organized the Jefferson Territory without the sanction of Congress. The wildness of this newly settled frontier was, of course, the stuff of legend and became the basis for countless books and later films. The gunslinging, hangman's-nooses-dangling-from-trees, high-noon-shootout antics so deeply rooted in the American psyche have a firm basis in the Pikes Peak Gold Rush. Bars, brothels, and gambling were cornerstones of the economy. Horace Greeley, editor of the *New York Tribune*, perhaps explained it best when he stated that there were "more brawls, more fights, more pistol-shots with criminal intent in this log city [Denver] of one hundred and fifty dwellings, not three-fourths completed nor two-thirds inhabited, nor one-third fit to be, than in any community of equal numbers on earth."

The extralegal Jefferson Territory came to an abrupt end in 1861. After the election of Abraham Lincoln prompted the secession of six slave states, the U.S. Congress, with fewer Southern senators to stop them, acted to increase the political power of the free states by admitting the eastern portion of the Territory of Kansas to the Union. This left the western portion of Kansas, including Denver and the mountain gold camps, unorganized. Congress quickly crafted a bill to create the Territory of Colorado, which was admitted to the Union as another free territory in 1861. Those original boundaries of Colorado remain unchanged today. Following the establishment of the Territory of Colorado, many attempts were made to gain statehood for the new territory, but not until 1876—exactly one hundred years after the United States declared its independence—was Colorado admitted to the union, earning it the nickname "the Centennial State."

Denver grew into a bustling supply center for nearby mining towns and had ambitious plans to turn itself into the largest and most prosperous city of the entire Rocky Mountain region, but Denver had a problem—it lay in the middle of nowhere. It was an island of civilization amid the vast wilderness of the High Plains and Rocky Mountains, linked to the rest of the country by a weeklong journey of jolting stagecoach travel through dangerous territory. For Denver to emerge from the unmapped wilds of Colorado as an important city, it had to be linked to major U.S. metropolitan areas by rail.

Early Denverites faced numerous setbacks as they schemed to build their dusty town into a mighty metropolis. In 1863 a great fire burned much of Denver's business district to the ground. A flash flood the following year again devastated the town. During the Civil War, a Confederate army from Texas marched on the state, hoping to seize its goldfields for the Confederacy. A volunteer Union army was raised in Denver, and after making an epic trek through a blizzard along the Santa Fe Trail and arriving in New Mexico, they defeated Rebel troops in the decisive Battle of Glorieta Pass, often referred to as the "Gettysburg of the West." Shortly after the Civil War battle, an Indian war broke out. Denver's telegraph lines were torn down, and its wagon trains were attacked, preventing communication and food from reaching the struggling town.

But the early challenges Denver faced only served to strengthen the resolve of stalwart citizens determined to make sure that Denver would not just survive but thrive. With fires, floods, and wars behind it, the little city where the mighty Rockies rose up from the Great Plains set its full attention to the task ahead: linking Colorado to the rest of the nation by rail.

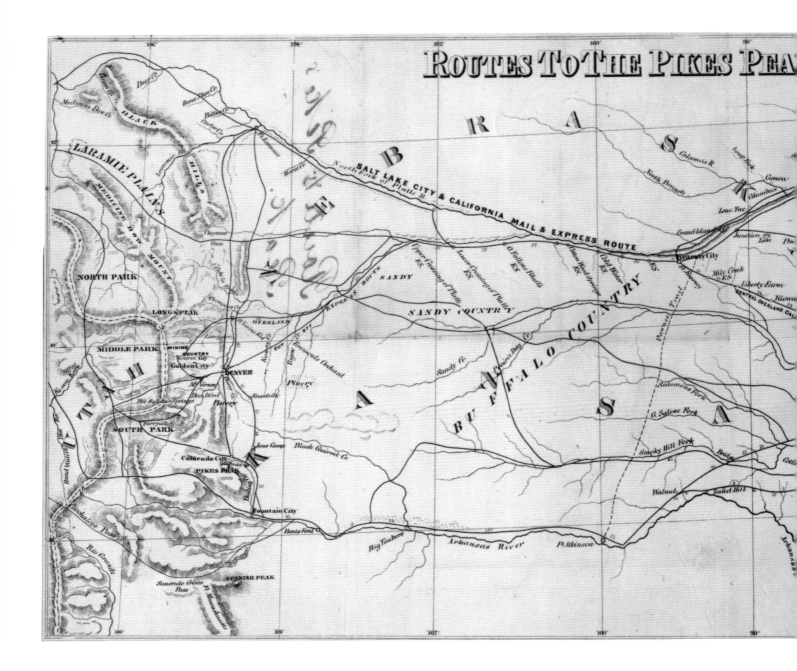

Routes to the Pikes Peak gold regions (186–).

As rumors of incredible wealth spread back east, easterners headed west in droves, blazing trails to the Colorado goldfields. The two main routes—the Platte River route (along the well-established Oregon Trail) and the Arkansas River route (along the heavily traveled Santa Fe Trail)—are illustrated here. Also depicted between the two main routes are secondary routes, whose proponents claimed were safer or more direct, such as the Smoky Hill Trail—though following these secondary routes often proved disastrous. Producers of maps depicting paths to

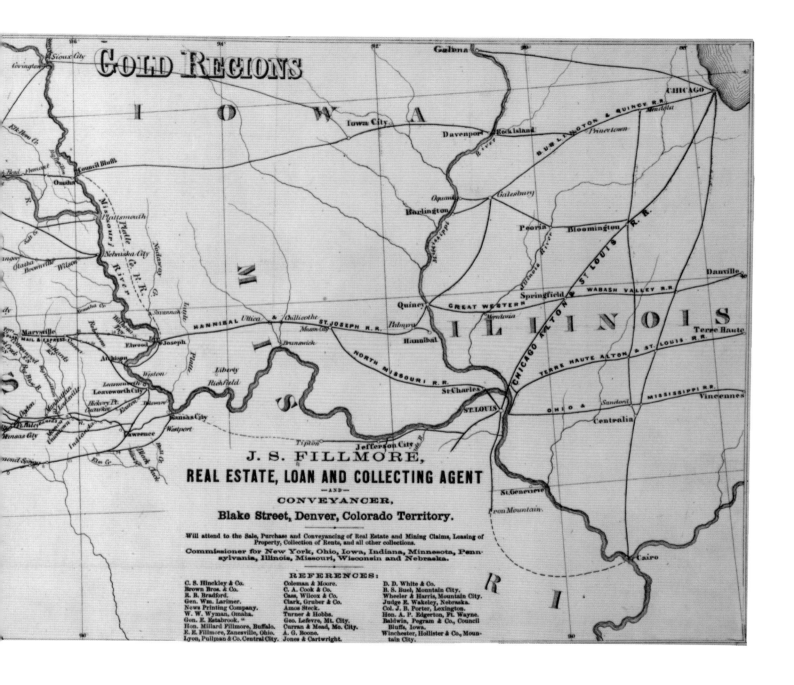

the goldfields weren't concerned as much about accuracy as they were about selling something. The maps had a commercial intent, whether it was to get gold seekers to travel a particular route so they would pass by a certain store on their way west, or to get as many people as possible to swarm to Denver so that real estate developers and loan agents—as in the case of this map—could cash in on the bonanza.

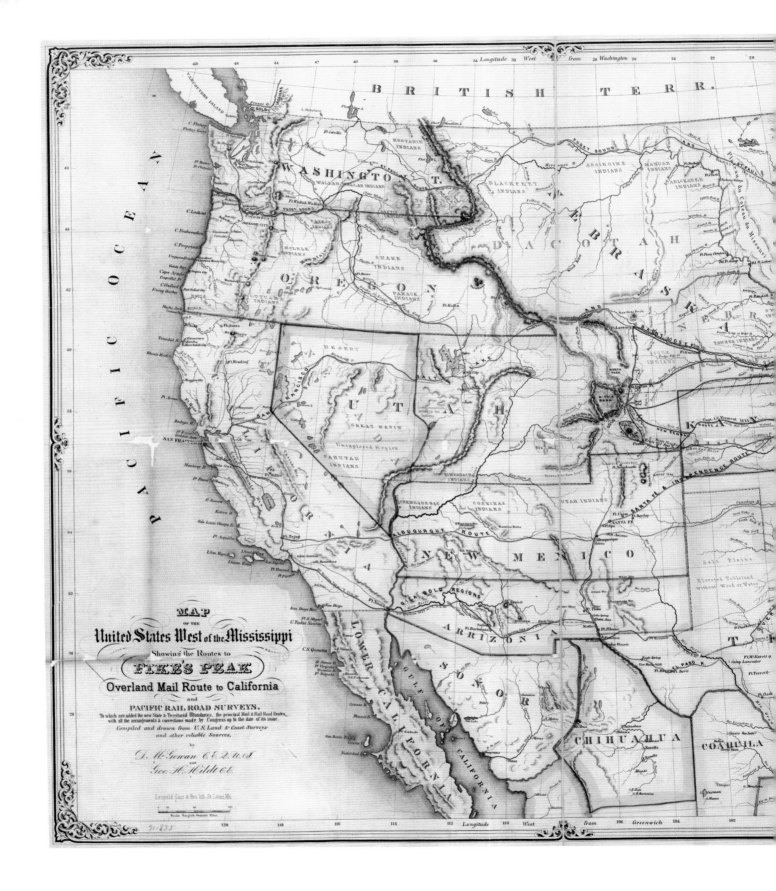

MAP
OF THE
United States West of the Mississippi
Showing the Routes to
PIKE'S PEAK
Overland Mail Route to California
and
PACIFIC RAIL ROAD SURVEYS,
To which are added the new State & Territorial Boundaries, the principal Mail & Rail Road Routes,
with all the arrangements & corrections made by Congress up to the date of its issue.
Compiled and drawn from U.S. Land & Coast Surveys
and other reliable Sources,
by
D. McGowan C.E. & U.S.
and
Geo. H. Hildt C.E.

Map of the United States west of the Mississippi showing the routes to Pike's Peak, overland mail route to California and Pacific rail road surveys. To which are added the new state & territorial boundaires [sic], the principal mail & rail road routes with all the arrangements & corrections made by Congress up to the date of its issue. Compiled and drawn from U.S. land & coast surveys and other reliable sources, by D. McGowan and Geo. H. Hildt (1859).

The Jefferson Territory was a short-lived and unsuccessful attempt to establish a government in the unorganized regions depicted on this map, which were rife with lawlessness and rapidly filling up with fortune seekers and settlers heading to the Pikes Peak goldfields. The provisional Jefferson Territory came to an end when Congress created the Colorado Territory with the present-day boundaries of Colorado in 1861. It was carved out of four surrounding territories: Utah Territory included all of present-day Colorado west of the Continental Divide; Nebraska, Kansas, and New Mexico Territories included parts of present-day Colorado east of the Continental Divide.

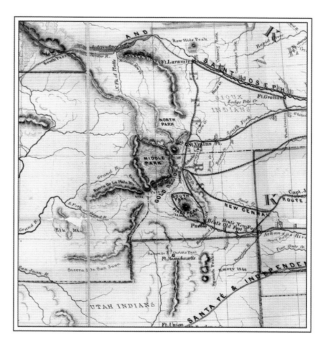

Map of Colorado Territory embracing the Central Gold Region, drawn by Frederick J. Ebert; under direction of the Governor Wm. Gilpin (1862).

Produced under the direction of William Gilpin, the first governor of the Colorado Territory and a passionate Colorado booster, this was one of the first commercial maps created of Colorado by itself after it became a territory. It was intended to promote the new territory and increase immigration into Colorado. The map shows the vast empty counties on the eastern plains and the Western Slope, and it gives a good indication of the state's settlement pattern. Denver, Boulder, and other major towns arose near the Front Range foothills of the Rockies, where rivers spill out of canyons onto the plains, providing water for agriculture and industry. The climate is relatively mild compared to the frigid high country to the west and the burning expanse of the Great Plains farther east. These Front Range towns formed the start of Colorado's urbanization, providing the core of permanent settlement. They swelled into cities and remained the state's main population centers as they supplied the mountain mining camps depicted on this map, many of which disappeared when the riches ran out.

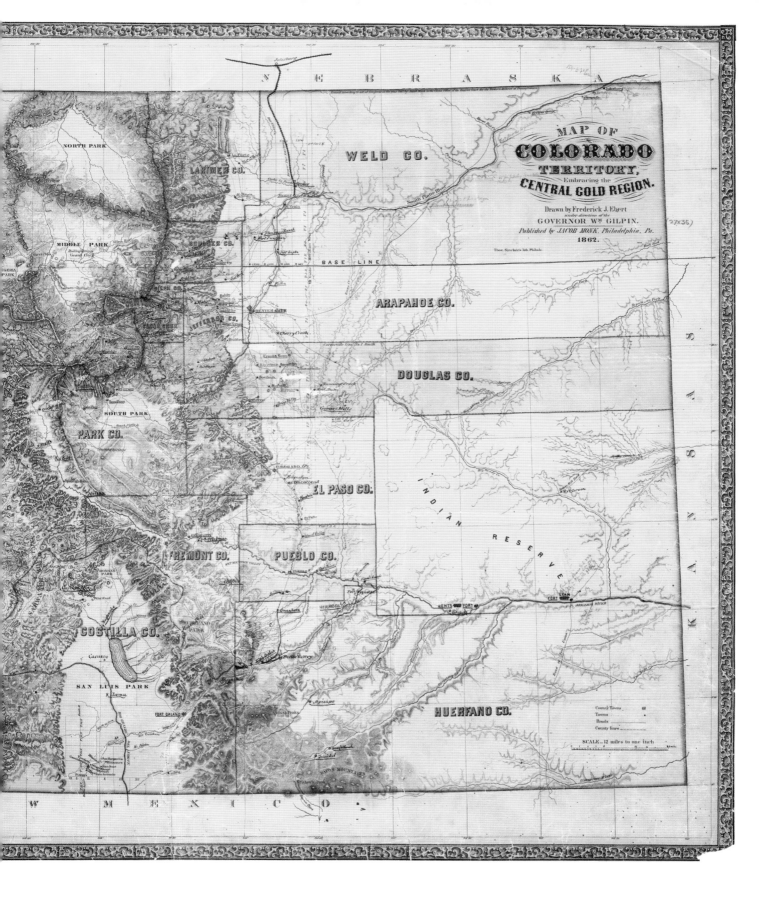

MAP OF
COLORADO
TERRITORY,
Embracing the
CENTRAL GOLD REGION.

Drawn by Frederick J. Ebert
under direction of the
GOVERNOR Wm GILPIN.
Published by JACOB MONK, Philadelphia, Pa.
1862.

Thos. Sinclair's lith. Philada.

N E B R A S K A

WELD CO.

LARIMER CO.

NORTH PARK

MIDDLE PARK

ARAPAHOE CO.

DENVER CITY

BASE LINE

DOUGLAS CO.

PARK CO.

SOUTH PARK

EL PASO CO.

INDIAN RESERVE

FREMONT CO.

PUEBLO CO.

COSTILLA CO.

SAN LUIS PARK

FORT GALAND

HUERFANO CO.

BENTS FORT

FORT LYON

ARKANSAS RIVER

K A N S A S

N E W   M E X I C O

County Towns
Towns
Roads
County lines

SCALE, 12 miles to one inch

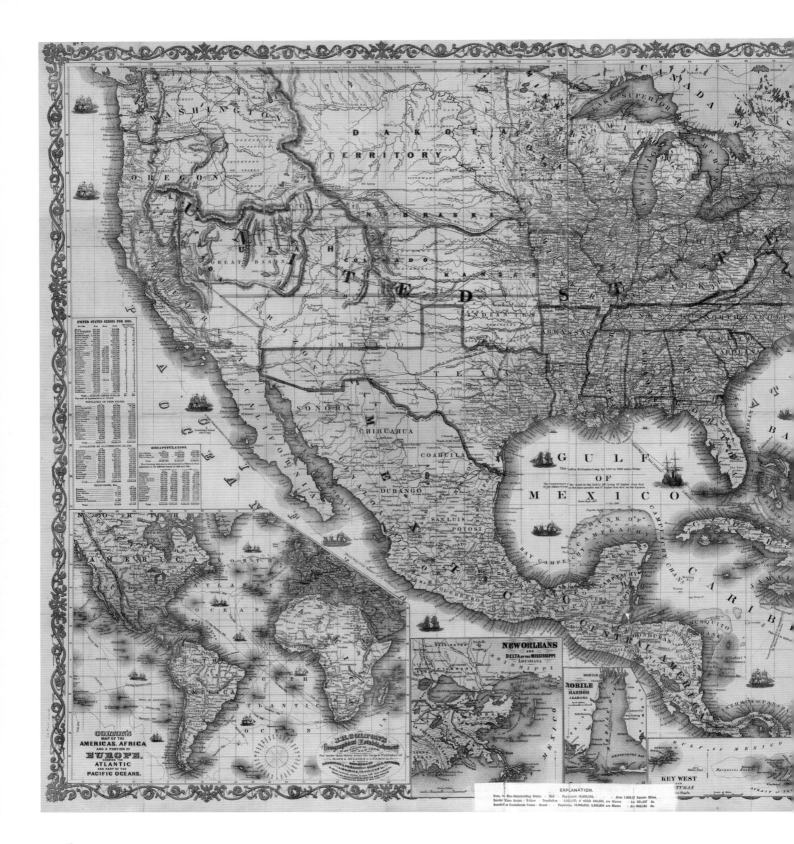

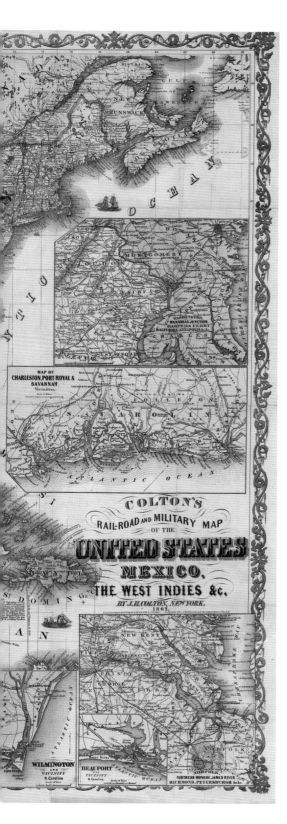

Colton's rail-road and military map of the United States, Mexico, the West Indies, &c. (1862).

Prior to the Civil War, the Territory of Colorado was formed by the U.S. Congress to increase the political power of free states in the Union. Though harboring some Confederate sympathizers, the Colorado Territory was part of the Union, as illustrated on this map. The events of the Civil War, including the Confederacy's attempt to gain control of its goldfields, stalled Colorado's plans to build railroads and achieve statehood. To stop Confederate troops in New Mexico from invading Colorado, a volunteer Union infantry marched from Bent's Fort, crossed Raton Pass (labeled "Pass of the Raton" on this map), and defeated Confederate forces at Glorieta Pass, southeast of the city of Santa Fe.

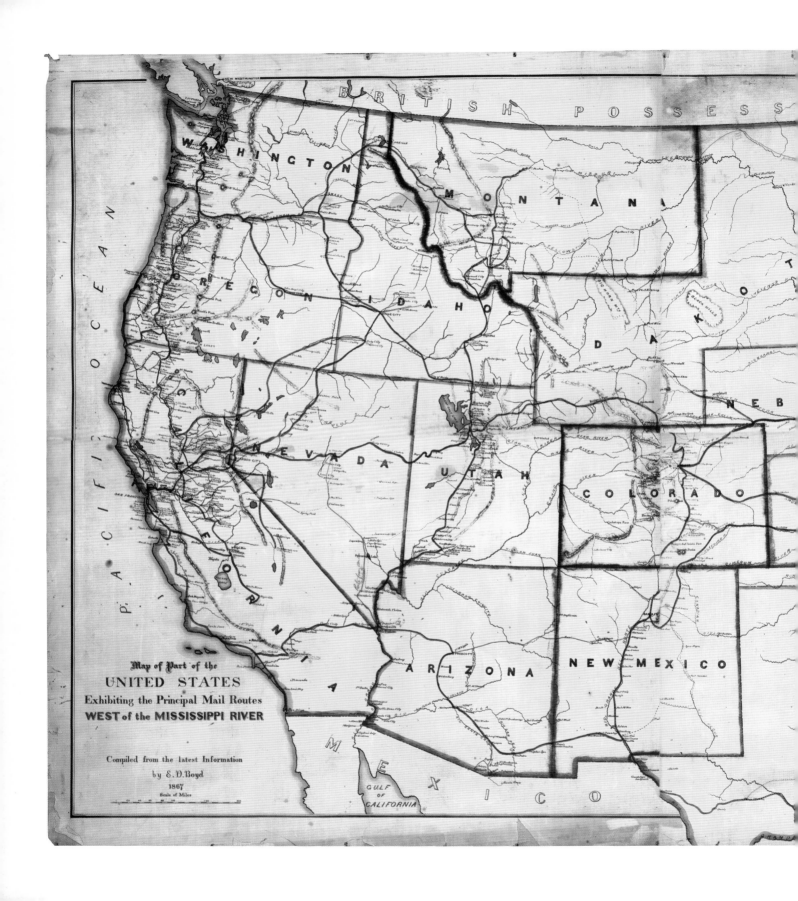

Map of Part of the
UNITED STATES
Exhibiting the Principal Mail Routes
WEST of the MISSISSIPPI RIVER

Compiled from the latest Information
by E. D. Boyd
1867
Scale of Miles

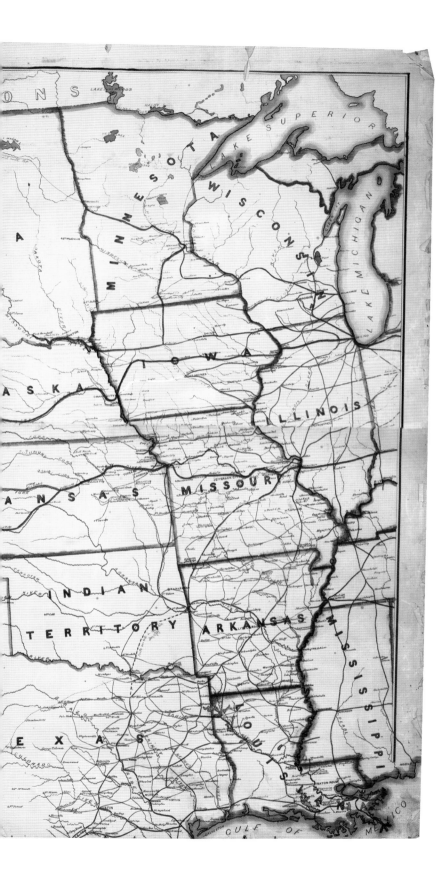

Denver, located at the edge of empty, arid plains along the foot of a forbidding mountain range, seemed an unlikely place for a city to grow, but beginning with the Pikes Peak Gold Rush, it became the economic hub and population center of the state. Denver was also Colorado's main point of connection to the rest of the country, through stagecoach lines, mail routes (as indicated on this map), telegraph routes, and, eventually, railroads. This map illustrates the formidable barrier the Colorado Rockies created to communication and transportation—routes flowed around the Colorado mountains, following the paths of least resistance.

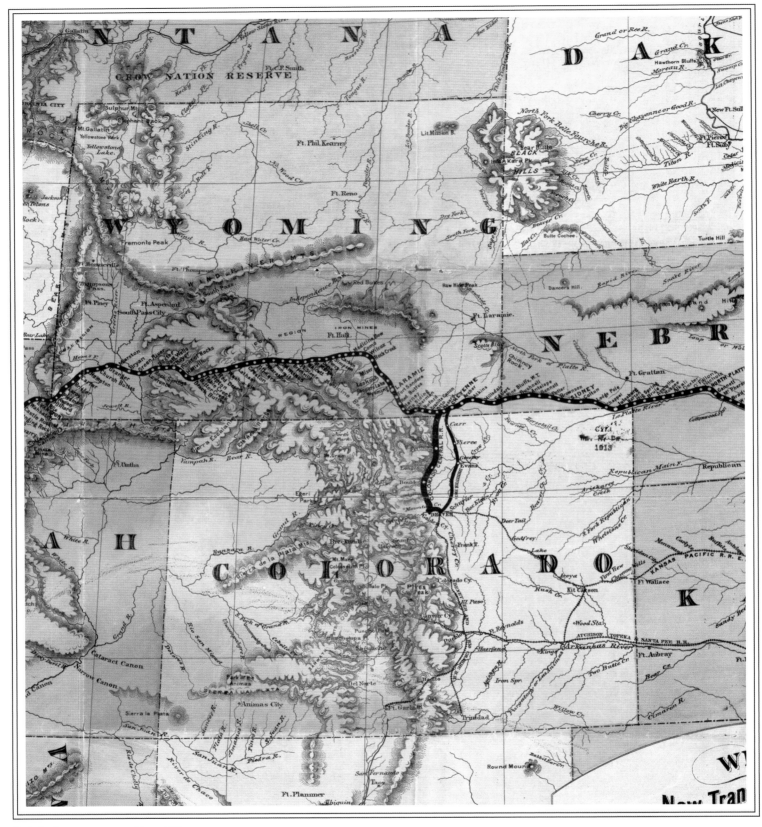

Detail of map on pages 54 and 55

Railroads

Denver's boosters assured railroad builders that the Rocky Mountains to the west of Denver were just gentle hills that could be easily traversed. But the Union Pacific, when planning its transcontinental route, very sensibly chose to bypass Colorado in favor of Cheyenne, Wyoming, and its relatively flat terrain, dashing Denver's hopes to "capture the iron horse." Businessmen and investors left Denver in droves, assuming Denver would disappear, and Colorado would remain a wild frontier. Some stubborn Denver supporters, however, raised funds to construct a Denver Pacific Railroad line to link Denver to the Transcontinental Railroad. Congress agreed to donate 900,000 acres of land for the railroad right-of-way, which allowed the Denver Pacific to secure loans and to press ahead with laying a hundred miles of tracks running from Denver to Cheyenne. Golden, Denver's main rival for the claim of Colorado's "Queen City," got in on the act and began building its own line to link it to the transcontinental route. Denver's determination paid off when rails joining Denver to the transcontinental line in Cheyenne were completed in June of 1870, and the iron horse roared through town, ushering in an era of vigorous growth for Colorado.

Two months after the Denver Pacific line with Cheyenne was completed, the Kansas Pacific railroad reached Denver, linking the rising Colorado town with the urban centers of Kansas City and St. Louis. This milestone ensured that Golden, which had yet to complete its railroad, or any other rival town that dared to question Denver's supremacy, would not take the spotlight away from the city that had, through much sweat and clever maneuvering, positioned itself to claim center stage in the drama of settlement taking place in the state.

In 1870 yet another major Colorado railroad was born. The Denver and Rio Grande (or, more commonly, the "Rio Grande") was created to link Denver to El Paso, Texas, to the south; through El Paso's connections, ultimately, it would join Denver to Mexican railroads. This ambitious plan marked a turning point for Denver: instead of struggling to connect to major railroad lines that had bypassed it, Denver was boldly building its own railroad with itself at the center. The Rio Grande plan called for a north-south main line, with feeder lines running west to the mountain mining camps and east to agricultural communities on the plains. The line's north-south orientation was a radical departure from other western railroads, which generally ran east-west. In addition, the line was designed to be built on narrow-gauge track instead of the standard-width track in use at the time. The narrow tracks, which allowed for laying rails in challenging mountainous terrain, proved such a success they eventually became the standard for railroads running through Colorado's mountains.

The Denver, South Park, and Pacific Railway, founded in 1872, used narrow-gauge tracks to ascend the rugged Platte Canyon to the west of Denver, traverse South Park, and then reach the mountain mining towns of Breckenridge, Dillon, and Keystone. In the same year the Colorado Central Railroad pushed its way up Clear Creek Canyon to the thriving mining district around Central City. Small locomotives chugged up steep, narrow-gauge tracks, causing the price of food and supplies to drop dramatically in mineral-rich regions throughout Colorado. Mountain lines were often laid along extremely tortuous routes in order to follow natural points of weakness, such as passes and gorges. The

long, winding lines allowed mines to transport their valuable ore, and they allowed Denver, with access to fuel and labor, to flourish as a smelting center. Within three years of connecting itself to the transcontinental line, Denver tripled its population and its business. The trains that rolled into Denver during the 1870s were loaded with precious metals and coal, and boomtown Denver built a steel spiderweb of rails to profit from the Rocky Mountain region's vast mining, farming, and ranching riches. Denver became, as its ambitious boosters had always hoped it would be, the rail hub of the Rockies, and it soon turned into the major industrial powerhouse of the High Plains. A hundred trains or more a day steamed in and out of Denver's Union Station, and smelter smoke hung over the city, signaling its prosperity.

In the 1880s the pace of railroad building accelerated at breakneck speed as railroad companies raced to lay track through strategic passes and link themselves to lucrative mining camps. All across the state, trestles were raised and tunnels were blasted. The railroad companies' sprint to reach the riches in the mountains was as frenzied as that of the gold-rush prospectors who'd headed into the hills with picks and pans. Major railroads—such as the Burlington, the Rock Island, and the Missouri Pacific—built from the east into Colorado, linking it with the rest of the nation's economy and fueling growth in the fledgling state. As these companies laid track throughout the eastern plains, railroad towns sprang up along their lines, and homesteaders filled the prairie.

Railroads eliminated Colorado's transportation problems, ended its isolation, and pumped enormous amounts of money through the state's economy—but the railroads came with a price. Much of the financing of the lines had come from outside the state, and control of the railroads lay not with the Colorado towns they ran through but with far-off investors who cared not at all about Colorado's progress or prosperity and who were concerned solely with their own profits. As tracks formed an ever-expanding grid across the state, citizens grumbled about being an economic colony of business interests in the East, and towns bypassed by the railroads withered and died. Nevertheless, iron horses raced along the new steel rails of Colorado, changing the landscape, economy, and culture of the state at a blistering pace.

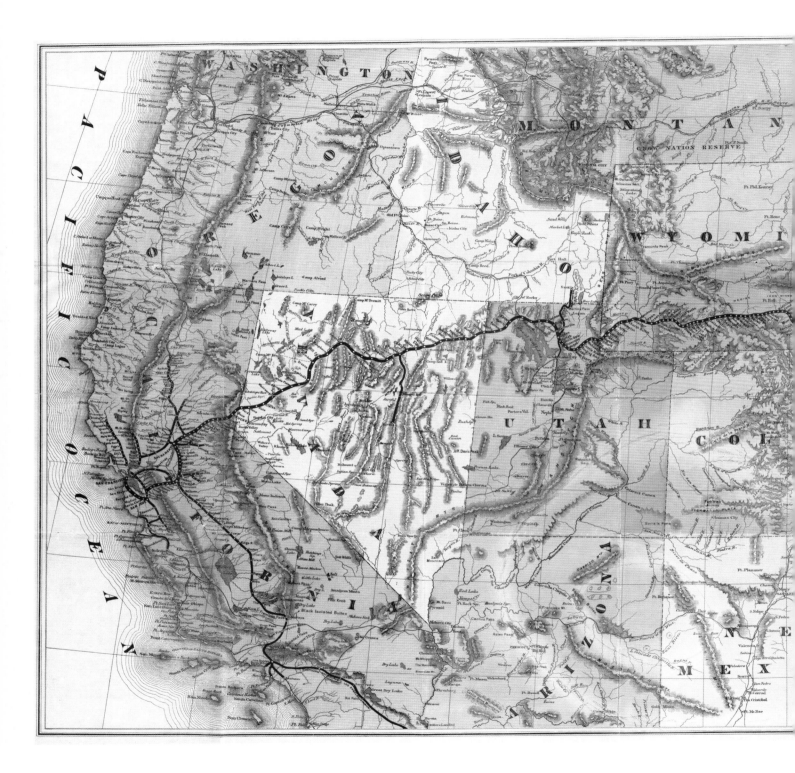

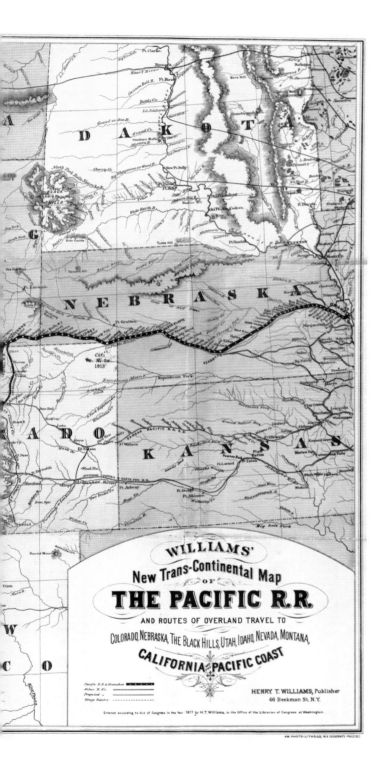

New trans-continental map of the Pacific R.R. and routes of overland travel to Colorado, Nebraska, the Black Hills, Utah, Idaho, Nevada, Montana, California, and the Pacific Coast (1877).

The year 1870, when Denver joined itself to the Transcontinental Railroad, has been called "the proudest year in the whole history of Denver," as it marked the end of a daunting challenge for the city to save itself from isolation and ushered in an era of tremendous growth and prosperity. The Denver Pacific line—the first line built to connect Colorado to the Union Pacific transcontinental railroad at Cheyenne, Wyoming—is shown here. The Colorado Central line, which a few years later tied Golden into the Transcontinental Railroad at Cheyenne, is also depicted.

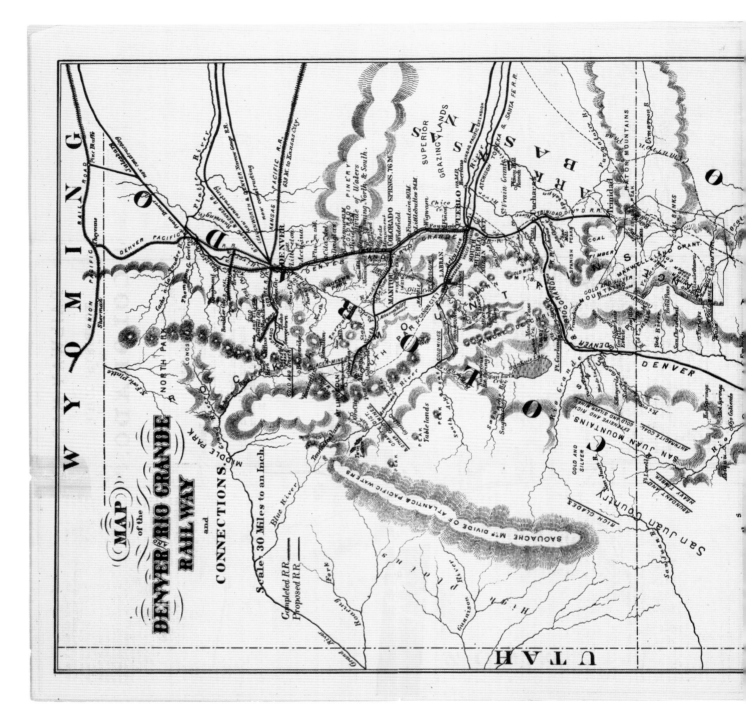

Map of the Denver and Rio Grande Railway and connections (1873).

This map, created as part of a report for Denver and Rio Grande stockholders, was most likely also used as a promotional piece for prospective investors and potential Colorado settlers. It illustrates the grand plan of the railroad's founder, General William Jackson Palmer, an ardent advocate for Colorado and a railroad visionary

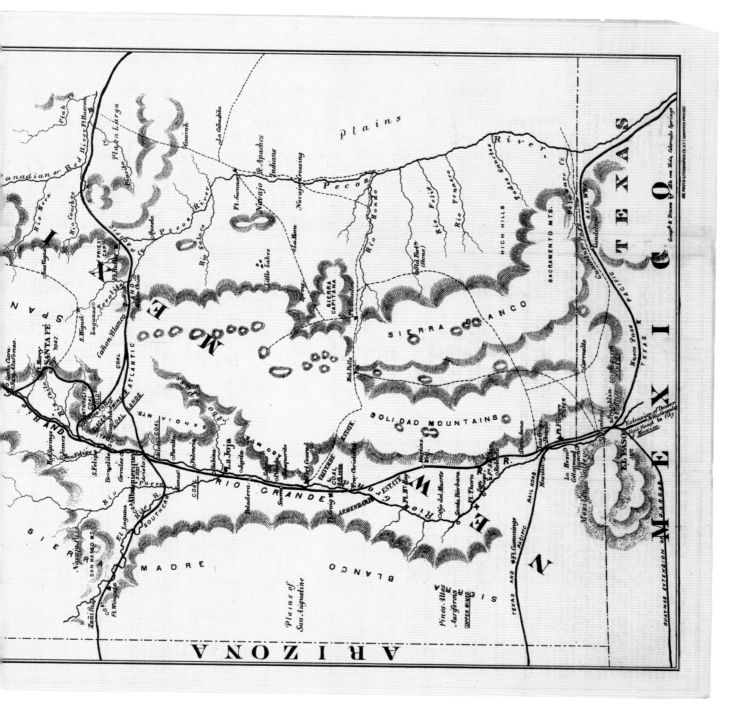

who created a regional rail system along the eastern base of the Rocky Mountains. Palmer planned to have every Colorado mining district connect to the main line, which would eventually extend all the way to Mexico City. Completed and proposed lines are indicated on this map. Note the north-south orientation of the main line, a major departure from the east-west orientation of other railroads in the western United States.

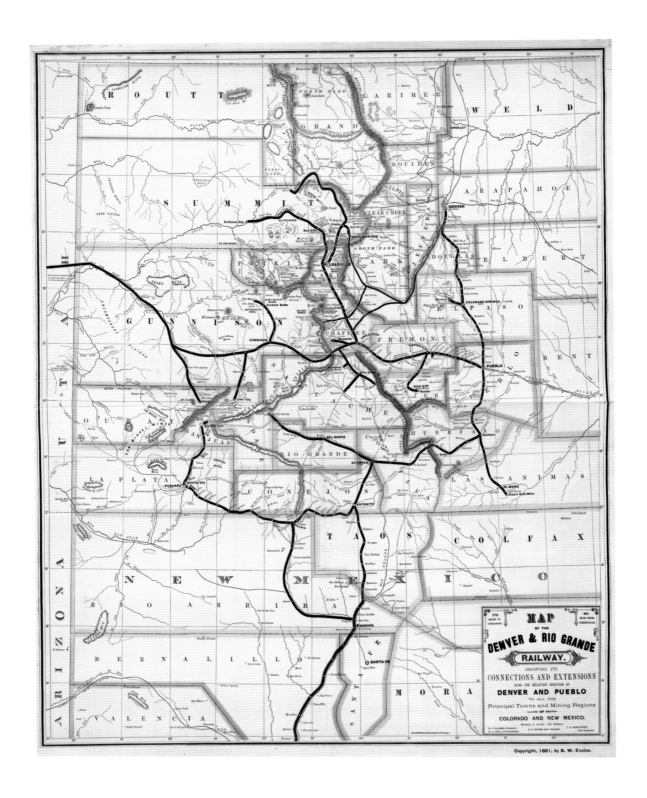

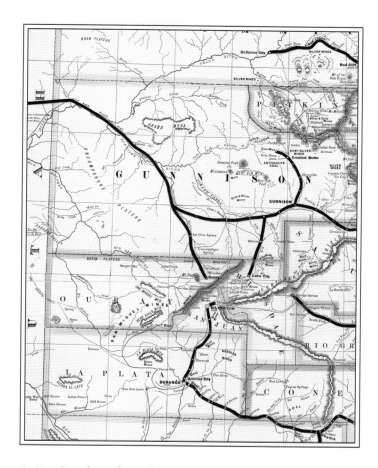

Map of the Denver & Rio Grande Railway, showing its connections and extensions also the relative position of Denver and Pueblo to all the principal towns and mining regions of Colorado and New Mexico (1881).

The tremendous growth of the Rio Grande Railway allowed commerce to flourish and towns to grow throughout Colorado in places bypassed by other railroads. The Rio Grande strayed from its southern focus and headed west when it lost a battle to the Santa Fe Railroad over control of Raton Pass into New Mexico and silver rushes in the Colorado mountains caught its attention. It laid track to the Front Range town of Cañon City and then followed the Arkansas River upstream all the way to Leadville to tap the silver riches there. The Rio Grande pushed lines through the most rugged parts of the Colorado Rockies by laying rails at altitudes higher than any that had been railroaded before. It was able to push its main line west to the confluence of the Grand (later renamed Colorado) and Gunnison Rivers, joining the budding west-slope metropolis of Grand Junction to Denver. The Rio Grande continued building west to Salt Lake City, a railroad gateway to California. The Rio Grande's vigorous development created a colossal network of trunk lines and spur lines totaling nearly 1,500 miles. Note the meandering routes on the map caused by the convoluted topography of the mountains. The motto of the Rio Grande was "Through the Rockies, not around them." Eventually, the Rio Grande took over a railroad line that had punched a 6.2-mile-long bore, known as the Moffat Tunnel, through the Continental Divide, allowing Rio Grande trains to travel due west from Denver to Salt Lake City and onward to California.

Indexed map of Colorado showing the railroads in the state, and the express company doing business over each, also counties and rivers (1879).

By the time this map was made, eastern Colorado was well served by several major rail lines, many routes had been pushed into mountain mining regions, and rails were beginning to penetrate the wilderness of western Colorado. Major lines such as the Denver Pacific, the Rio Grande, and the Kansas Pacific are named here, as are lesser-known lines, such as the Colorado Central, that flourished briefly and then were either abandoned or absorbed into the larger matrix of major railroads. In terms of how it was created, this map marks a turning point: The color on the map was printed rather than applied by hand, and the map was produced using a wax-engraving method. As books other than Bibles began to proliferate in American homes, wax engraving, less expensive than engraving metal plates and much easier to update, made it possible to produce maps on a scale that could meet increasing demand. But the care taken to create a beautiful object that went with engraving metal plates and hand applying color was disappearing. Eventually, as cars replaced trains and rails gave way to roads, a lithographic process became the standard for mass-produced maps, and the craftsmanship evident in early Colorado cartography became a thing of the past.

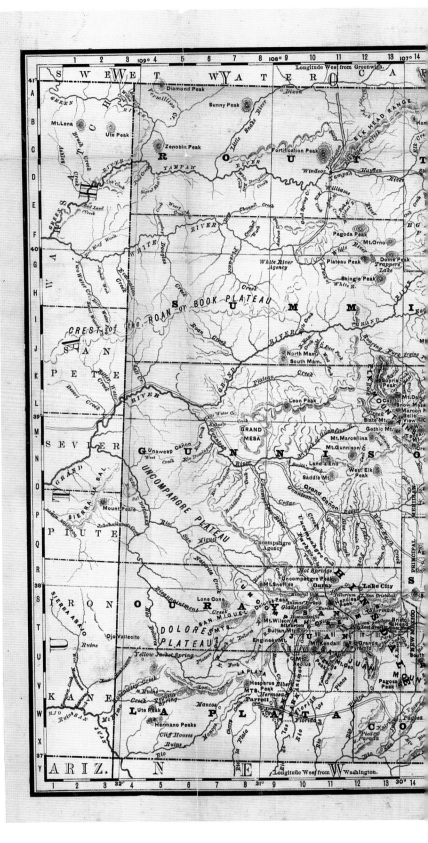

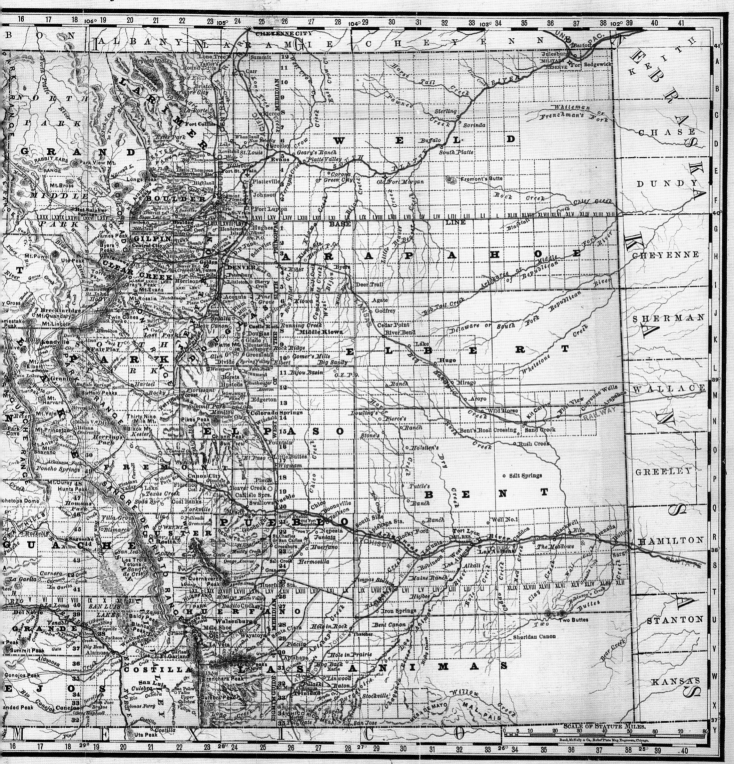

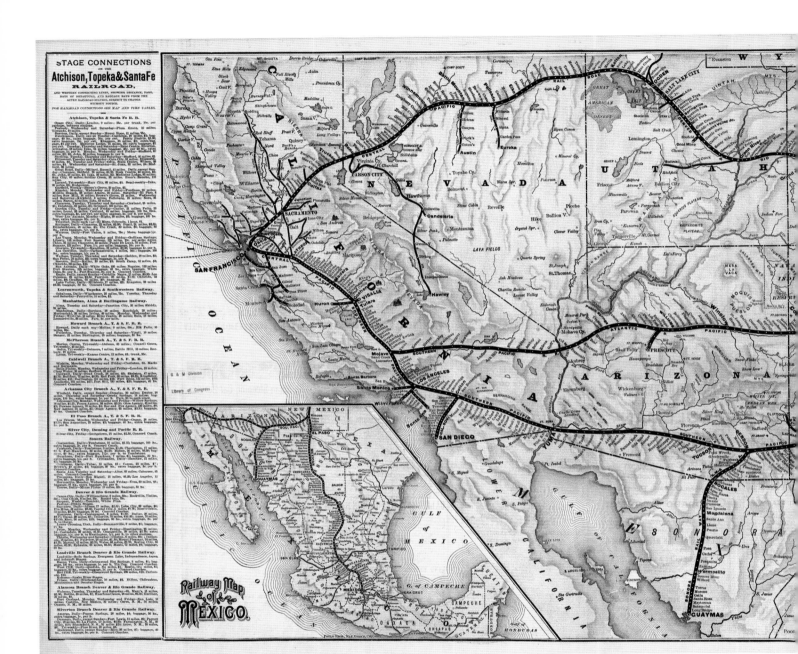

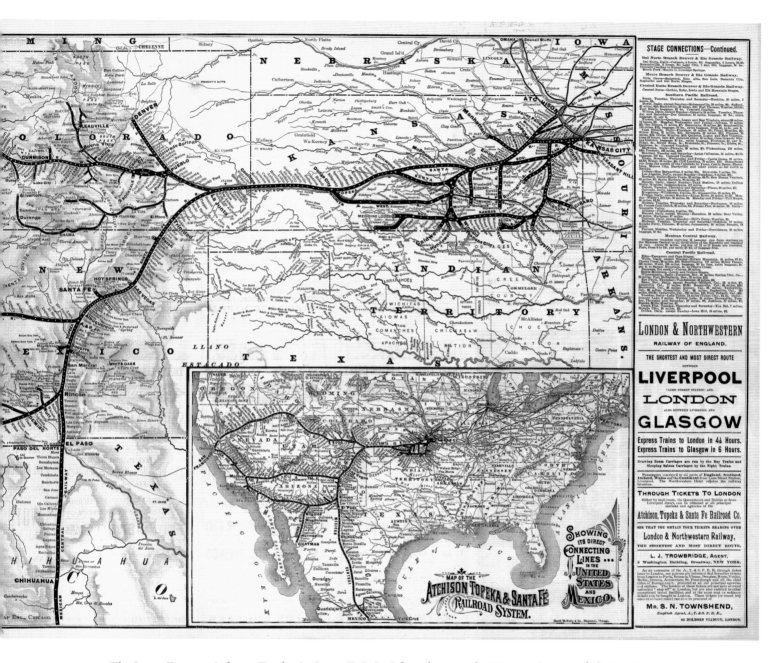

MAP OF THE
ATCHISON TOPEKA & SANTA FE
RAILROAD SYSTEM.

SHOWING ITS DIRECT CONNECTING LINES ... IN THE UNITED STATES AND MEXICO.

The Santa Fé route Atchison, Topeka & Santa Fé R.R. 3 lines between the Missouri River and the Pacific coast to the city of Mexico via the A.T.&S. and Mexican Central R.R. (1884).

The Atchison, Topeka and Santa Fe Railway ("the Santa Fe") laid tracks to the Kansas-Colorado state line in 1873, and after connecting to Pueblo in 1876, it began hauling Colorado coal eastward. After heated competition with the Denver and Rio Grande Railroad, which escalated into the Royal Gorge Railroad War, and surmounting the physical challenge of building across the Rockies, the Santa Fe succeeded in laying a line across Colorado. Soon it ran a track all the way to California, adding yet another major rail line to Colorado's ever-expanding network and allowing the state more access to markets for its products and more opportunities for town building and population expansion.

HOW THE PUBLIC DOMAIN HAS BEEN SQUANDERED

Map showing the **139,403,026** acres of the people's land—equal to

871,268 FARMS OF 160 ACRES EACH

Worth at $2 an acre, $278,806,052,

GIVEN BY

Republican Congresses to Railroad Corporations

This is more land than is contained in New York, New Jersey, Pennsylvania, Ohio, and Indiana.

We believe that the public lands ought, as far as possible, to be kept as homesteads for actual settlers; that all unearned lands heretofore improvidently granted to railroad corporations by the action of the Republican party should be restored to the public domain; and that no more grants of land shall be made to corporations, or be allowed to fall into the ownership of alien absentees.

DEMOCRATIC PLATFORM, 1884.

How the public domain has been squandered, map showing the 139,403,026 acres of the people's land—equal to 871,268 farms of 160 acres each, worth at $2 an acre, $278,806,052, given by Republican Congresses to railroad corporations, Rand, McNally & Co., Engr's. Chicago (1884).

The railroads put an end to Colorado's isolation and proved a tremendous financial boon for the majority of Colorado's citizens, but the railroads were not without controversy, as this angry map illustrates. After being awarded land grants by Congress long after transcontinental tracks had been laid across the West, railroad companies opened real estate offices to sell their grants as farmland. The new farms they sold needed freight and passenger transportation, which was, conveniently, provided by the railroads, many of which made fortunes from the land awarded to them and created railroads that the nation didn't necessarily need. Shenanigans such as these often incensed the public, which began to view the railroad land grants as gratuitous giveaways to big business instead of a necessary means to develop critical national infrastructure for the public good.

Town Building

In 1851 San Luis, the first permanent non-Indian settlement in Colorado, was founded on the Culebra River, a tributary of the Rio Grande in the San Luis Valley. This agricultural community survived amid Colorado's harsh terrain, but town building in the state really didn't take off until Anglo-Americans began flooding into Colorado in search of precious metal and railroads laid their tracks across the mountains and the plains.

Denver's population in 1880 stood at 35,000. Twenty years later, in 1900, it had increased to nearly 134,000, making Denver the second-most-populous city in the West, second only to San Francisco. Denver earned the nickname "Queen City of the Plains" as it underwent impressive expansion. New streets and cable car systems were built, creating commuter suburbs and establishing Denver as the dominant urban area in the Rocky Mountain region. This new metropolis of the West boasted electric lights, electric streetcars, and telephones. It had the best theaters, schools, and hospitals in Colorado, as well as the state's richest banks. Sprawling mansions were erected on Denver's posh Capitol Hill, and a handsome opera house and ornate hotels sprang up downtown as the city continued to boom.

A similar population explosion happened in other areas of the state. Colorado's railroad construction, by helping to stimulate the state's farming industry, spur the growth of gargantuan cattle ranches, and encourage an influx of settlers, led to the creation of dozens of railroad towns. While track was being laid across Colorado, an innovation in agriculture occurred that had perhaps as profound an effect on the Colorado economy, the development of its towns, and the distribution of its population as that of the Pikes Peak Gold Rush or the arrival of the railroad: Water was diverted from streams to irrigate the "Great American Desert." Land that had been deemed uninhabitable bloomed, leading to the formation of towns along the parched eastern plains and the state's scorched western plateau.

Nathan Meeker, the agriculture editor of the *New York Tribune*, heeded the advice of his editor Horace Greeley, who declared in an editorial, "go West young man, ..." West Meeker went, arriving on Colorado's eastern prairie and founding Union Colony, a utopian community based on cooperation, temperance, religion, and—perhaps most important—irrigation. The system of canals that was constructed allowed Meeker's town to flourish, and it became a model for other Colorado settlements upon the High Plains.

On the opposite side of the state, after the Rio Grande Railroad laid tracks through the small town of Grand Junction on Colorado's Western Slope, hotels, saloons, blacksmith shops, and lumber mills were established to provide services to the settlers who were pouring in. Canals were constructed to transport water from Grand Mesa and the Colorado River to surrounding areas, and thriving agricultural industries fueled the burgeoning region's economy.

Some towns grew due to factors other than railroads and irrigation agriculture. Boulder, for example, had been founded at the beginning of the Pikes Peak Gold Rush as a supply base for prospectors heading into the nearby mountains, providing them with mining equipment, housing, and entertainment. But the town moved away from its roots and began to grow into one of Colorado's most significant cities when a group of Boulder residents successfully lobbied to have the University of Colorado located in Boulder, changing the focus of the town from mining to education.

Though Colorado's economy was beginning to diversify, mineral booms were still the main engine powering the state's growth.

Fort Collins, Colorado (1865?).

Camp Collins was created by the U.S. Army in 1862 to protect travelers from attacks by hostile Plains Indians on the Overland Trail. Holding a handful of soldiers, Camp Collins was a tiny frontier outpost where the High Plains bumped up against the mountains. Following a devastating flood in 1864, the encampment was relocated to a section of high ground safe from the surging waters of the Cache la Poudre River. The new military base, which became known as Fort Collins, is depicted in this perspective map created by western artist Merritt Dana Houghton. The map shows soldiers assembled in a camp without walls (Fort Collins was never a walled fort); wagon trains traveling along the Overland Trail; and barracks, stables, guard houses, and storehouses built of log construction typical of the time and place. When the conflict between white settlers and Native Americans ended with all Plains Indians being removed from the Colorado Territory, the military post was abandoned. Savvy promoters subdivided the land, built a network of irrigation canals, and sold memberships that entitled purchasers to live on town lots and to raise crops on farming plots, transforming Fort Collins into one of Colorado's most successful agricultural settlements.

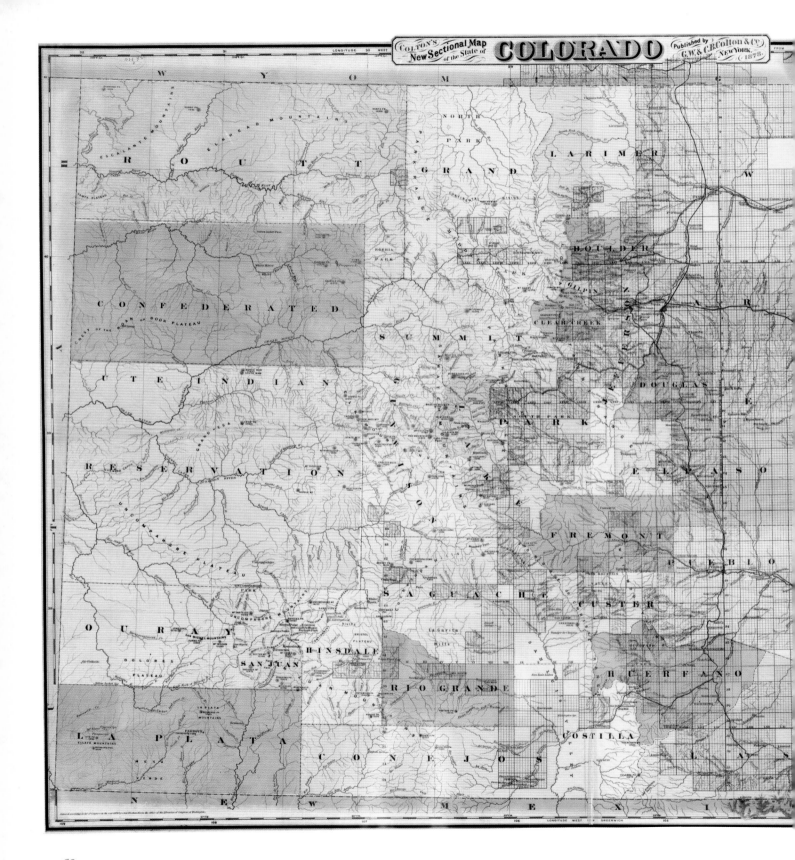

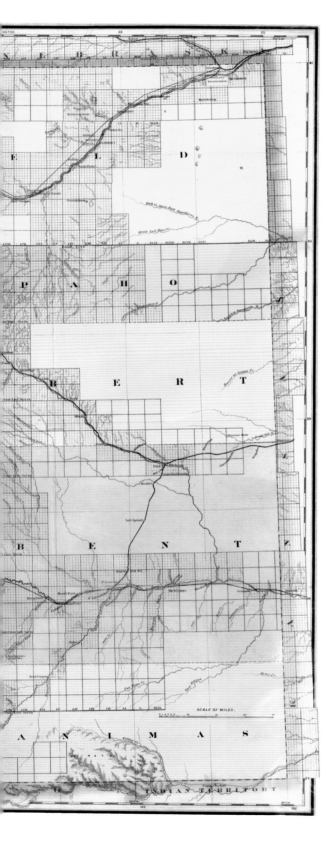

Colton's new sectional map of the state of Colorado (1878).

Joseph Hutchins Colton was part of a generation of cartographers and map publishers that defined American cartography in the mid- to late-nineteenth century. The Colton firm was taken over by Joseph's sons, who established the Colton company's reputation for accurately providing extensive information, on display in the fine craftsmanship of this map, which depicts Colorado's towns along its growing lifeline of railroads. The areas with grids indicate land that had been surveyed and was available for homesteading. When homesteaders started to fill the eastern plains, the enormous counties shown on this map that stretch from the Front Range all the way to the Kansas border eventually broke apart into smaller counties with prairie towns as their county seats that could handle the legal affairs of the new farming communities. At the time of this map's creation, populous mining towns in the mountains had carved small counties with nearby county seats out of the massive western counties that had appeared on earlier maps. The western counties were further split apart when the Utes were removed from western Colorado and new towns emerged. The counties on this map are hand colored to show the boundaries between them, a process that was tedious but produced beautiful results. This is one of the first maps of Colorado by itself after it achieved statehood in 1876.

Bird's eye view of the city of Denver, Colorado. Drawn by J. H. Flett (1881).

Nineteenth-century bird's-eye-view maps compressed industrial spaces and living spaces into compact, attractive scenes that graphically illustrated the vibrant life of Colorado's booming cities and towns during the Victorian era. Not drawn to scale, bird's-eye views, also known as perspective maps or panoramic maps, borrowed from a popular European cartographic technique to provide images of cities viewed at an oblique angle from an elevation of 2,000 to 3,000 feet above the ground. Bird's-eye-view maps were designed to show street patterns, buildings, and major landscape features in an idealized version of a town or city. Requiring painstakingly detailed labor to create, these maps began with a mapmaker drawing a frame that showed the pattern of streets in perspective. Then the mapmaker walked the streets, meticulously sketching homes, buildings, and features of the landscape to later add to the frame, eventually filling it with enough detail to provide a plausible representation of a town. Bird's-eye-view mapmakers sometimes added details that didn't exist, such as buildings that were planned but not yet constructed, to make a town appear more important or prosperous than it actually was. Often commissioned by a chamber of commerce or a real estate agency, these maps were used by promoters to increase population and to encourage commerce, and they were widely displayed on the walls of homes and businesses throughout Colorado as reminders of the state's rapid industrial development and economic growth. For a fee bird's-eye-map artists would include illustrations of private homes and businesses as separate insets so that proud citizens could point out their property on the maps. Handsome structures built from Denver's mining wealth are featured in the vignettes of this map, and the railroads that drove Denver's development are also evident here. The city's original Union Depot train station, which opened in 1881 and later was renamed Union Station after being rebuilt, is prominently displayed at the top of the map.

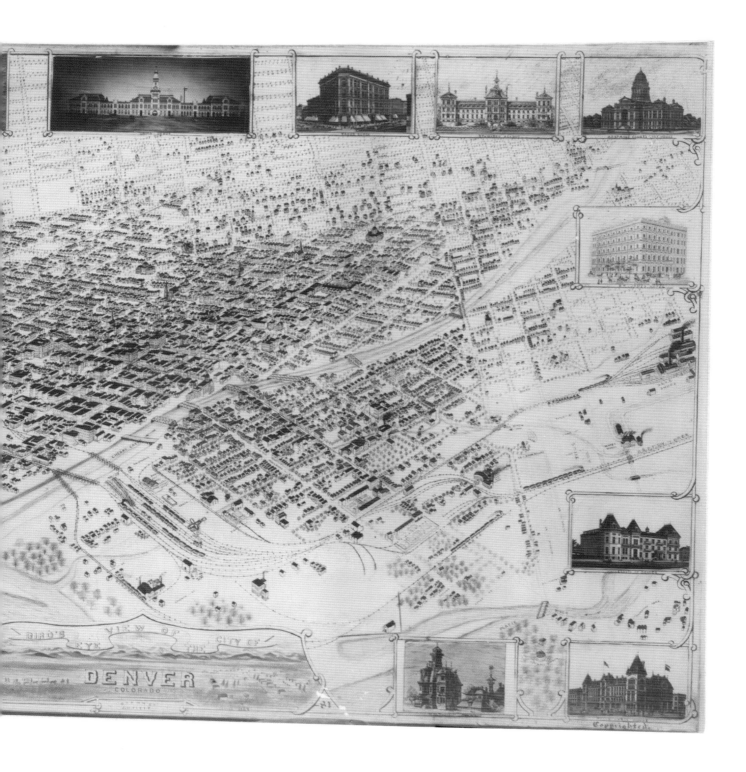

BIRD'S EYE VIEW OF THE CITY OF

DENVER
COLORADO

H. Waring, Fruits, Confectionery, etc., Main St.

B. F. Marsh, Photographer, Main St.

F. G. Fisher, Gunsmith, and Dealer in Fire Arms, Main St.

T. A. Kerr, Harness and Saddle Manufacturer, Main St.

Beetham & McDonald, Meat and Vegetable Market, Main St.

F. L. Childs, Groceries, Confectionery and Bakery, Main St.

J. E. Billings, Carriage Manufacturer, Cor. Madison Ave. & Walnut St.

Houghton & McElroy, Contractors and Builders, Madison Ave.

N. W. Hall & Co., Furniture and Hardware, Madison Ave.

J. F. Fezer, Drugs and Medicines, Main St.

Willard & Woodbury, Hardware and Furniture, Main St.

W. R. McClellan, Coal, Lime, Farm Produce and Agricultural Implements, Main St.

H. B. Jackson, Dry and Fancy Goods, Boots and Shoes, Hats and Caps, Groceries, etc., Madison Ave.

L. Roy Mansfield, Books and Stationery, News, and Musical Instruments, Main St.

A Presbyterian Church.
B Baptist Church.
C Congregational Church.
D Methodist Church.
E Episcopal Church.
F Greeley High School.
G Ward Schools.
H Oasis Hotel, J. F. Stafford, Prop'r.
J Exchange Hotel, Samuel Graham, Prop'r.
K Colorado House, H. N. Rogerson, Prop'r.

A. Z. Salomon, { Dry Goods and Clothing, Hats, Caps, Boots and Shoes, Madison Ave. Cor. Millinery and Fancy Goods, Maple St. Groceries, Provisions, Flour and Feed.

J. M. Freeman, Attorney at Law, Main St.

Jesse Hawes, Physician and Surgeon, Main St.

Scott, Attorney at Law, Main St.

Emerson & West, Bankers, Main St.

H. H. Barton, Jeweler, Main St.

Gipson & Nice, Attorneys at Law, Main St.

B. D. Sanborn, Insurance and Real Estate, Main St.

BIRD'S EYE VIEW OF

GREELEY, COLO.

COUNTY SEAT   OF WELD CO.

1882.

Copyright 1882 by J. J. Stoner, Madison, Wis.

W. M. Boomer,

H. A. French,

Caruer & Packa

J. D. Buckley,

R. L. Hall & C

Smith & Farr,

Camp & Nusba

Bird's eye view of Greeley, Colo. county seat
of Weld County. Beck & Pauli, lithographers (1882).
Union Colony was established by Nathan Meeker as a cooperative agricultural venture and utopian religious community. It served as a model for other agricultural colonies throughout Colorado and later became the city of Greeley, one of the state's largest population centers. This map's extensive index details the thriving commerce of the town, listing everything from shoe shops and vegetable markets to manufacturers of carriages, coffins, and violins.

ackson House.
reeley City Mills, B. F. Johnson.
arden City Mills, J. E. Graham & Co.
levator, J. L. Ewing & Co.
umber and Coal Yard, J. L. Ewing & Co.
eed and Planing Mill, C. W. Matteson & Son.
umber Yard, J. K. Thompson & Bro.
rick Yard, Jas. McAfee.
eed, Sale and Livery Stable, W. B. Wright.
eed, Sale and Livery Stable, Graham Bros.

Hair Dressing and Baths, Main St.
roprietor Colorado Sun, Madison Ave.
ad Proprietors Greeley Tribune, Maple St.
er, Main St.
s and Builders, Adams Ave. Cor. Maple St
d Wagon Shop, Walnut St.
ntractors.

W. A. Nichols, Groceries and Provisions, Main St.
Charles Brown, Boot and Shoe Shop, Main St.
Haynes, Dunning & Haynes, Attorneys at Law, Madison Ave.
H. P. Heath, Harness Manufacturer, Main St.
A. W. Tyroff, Merchant Tailoring, Madison Ave.
J. H Richardson, Manufacturer of Coffins, Carpenter and Builder,
    Maple St.
J. Joyce, Boot and Shoe Shop, Maple St.
A. A. Woodbury, Blacksmith and Wagon Shop, Walnut St.
L. von Ghoren, Real Estate and Notary, Walnut St.
Joseph Moore, Coal Dealer, Maple St.
Geo. W. Fisk, Manufacturer of Violins, Linden St.
F. H. Grove, Contractor and Builder, Walnut St.
Jos. Moss, Contractor and Builder, Grant Ave. Cor. Linden St.
Thos. Robbins, House and Sign Painting, Kalsomining and Paper
    Hanging, Walnut St.
Gale & Lee, Groceries, Provisions and Crockery, Main St.
J. M. McHenry, Brick Contractor, Cherry St.

1. Methodist Church.
2. Public School.
3. Empire Stamp Mill.
4. Polar Star Stamp Mill.
5. Black Hawk   "
6. Gregory   "
7. New York   "
8. Campbell & Peirce, Sampling Works.
9. Randolf Stamp Mill.

10. Independent Sampling Works.
11. Stamp Mill.
12. C. C. R. R. Depot.
13. Foundry and Mach. Shop, Silas Bertenshaw.
14. Carriage and Wagon Mfg., Boellert & Fick.
15. Black Hawk Boiler Works, Geo. Stroehle.
16. Pacific House, W. Feehan, Prop.
17. Mountain House, P. B. Wright, Prop.
18. Gregory House, M. McDonald, Prop.
19. Gregory Mine.

BLACK HA

I

LOOKING

Copyright 1882

Black Hawk, Colo. Beck & Pauli, lithographers (1882).
Black Hawk, in the heart of the state's bustling central mining region and linked to the Front Range town of Golden by the Colorado Central Railroad, grew into a thriving city complete with the state's first successful ore smelter. The smelters illustrated in the insets of this map helped to revolutionize hard-rock mining in Colorado

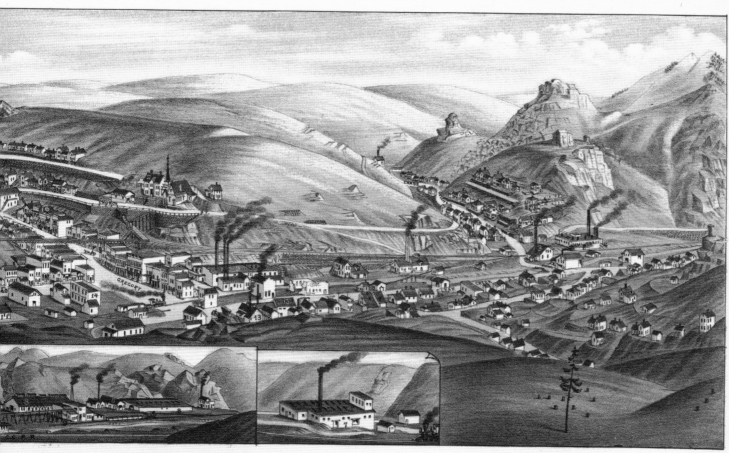

WK, COLO.

32.

TH EAST

Stoner, Madison, Wis.

Beck & Pauli, Lithographers, Milwaukee, Wis.

BUSINESS REFERENCES.

Sam Smith & Co., Bankers, Gregory St.
H. H. Stebbins & Co., Drugs and Chemicals, Gregory St
Mahr Mdse. Co., A. J. Smith, Manager,   "
Salisbury & Bertenshaw, Groceries & Provisions,   "
A. Ritmaster & Co., Dry Goods, Clothing, Boots, Shoes,
          etc., Gregory St.
Miller & Koch, Black Hawk, Cracker Works,   "
Anton Mehrlich, Saloon and Billiard Parlor,   "
R. H. Price, Groceries and Provisions,   "

Nels Kellerup, Saloon and Billiard Parlor,   "
J. Morrison, Merchant Tailoring,   "
G. S. Martin, Physician and Surgeon,   "
Gilpin Coal Feed and Lumber Co., Main St.
J. J. Hamilik, Meat Market, Main and Gregory Sts.
John Q. Griffith, Saloon and Billiard Parlor, Gregory St.
J. J. Loughran,   "   "   "   "
B. Olsen,   "   "   "   Main St.
Mrs. S. N. Hitchcock, Millinery,   "
D. H. Young's, House and Carriage Painter, Gregory St.

and led the way for massive mineral booms. But Denver eventually became the state's smelting center, and Black Hawk depopulated to a ghost town during mining busts. In the late twentieth century, a gambling boom raised new buildings in Black Hawk from the mining rubble.

Panoramic bird's eye view of Colorado Springs, Colorado City and Manitou, Colo. Beck & Pauli, lithographers (1882).

Colorado Springs was founded by railroad titan General William Jackson Palmer as a world-class resort community that Palmer declared should be free of saloons and other Wild West rowdiness and was "the most attractive place for homes in the West." The town's plethora of churches are on prominent display here, as are the lovely Victorian houses and hotels that lent Colorado Springs an air of elegance and refinement that was lacking in many of the coarse towns that sprang up around mineral booms. Because of the crowds of English tourists who enjoyed Colorado Springs, it was dubbed "Little London." Its biggest draw for tourists was a cog railroad that climbed to the summit of Pikes Peak. And for the tuberculosis sufferers who flocked to the area looking for relief from their symptoms, nearby mineral springs boosted their spirits, if not their health, and an abundance of clean, dry air soothed their ailing lungs. Named for the Algonquin word meaning "spirit," the charming town of Manitou Springs is depicted on this map; it became famous for its naturally carbonated, mineral-rich waters that bubble up from deep, underground aquifers. Also depicted is the anything-goes, rough-and-tumble town of Colorado City that Palmer, with his vision of high morals and sophisticated living, detested. Bird's-eye-view maps such as this one allowed potential transplants to see where vacant land was located for development and helped them understand business opportunities. For example, an entrepreneur searching for a major market to sell coal would most likely not locate an office in Colorado Springs because there are no smelters, but someone looking to start a tuberculosis hospital might study the map and see the lack of smelters as an asset.

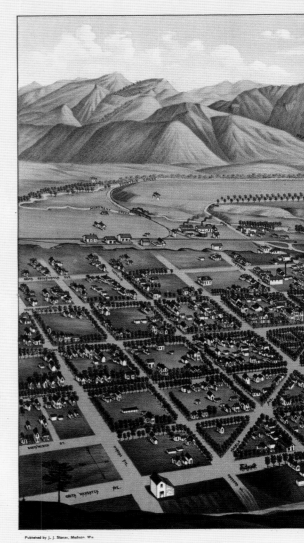

Published by J. J. Stoner, Madison, Wis.

1. Colorado College.
2. Blind and Deaf-Mute Institute.
3. High School and School Buildings.
4. Court House.
5. County Jail.
6. Opera House.
7. Gas Works.
8. D. & R. G. R. W. Depot.
9. Alamo Square or South Park.
10. Acacia Place, or North Park.
11. Fire Engine House.

CHURCHES.

12. Congregational Church.
13. Methodist Episcopal Church.
14. Presbyterian Church.
15. Baptist Church.
16. Episcopal Church.
17. M. E. South Church.
18. Christian Church.
19. R. Catholic Church.
20. Cumberland Presbyterian Church.
21. African Church.
22. Methodist Church, Colorado City.

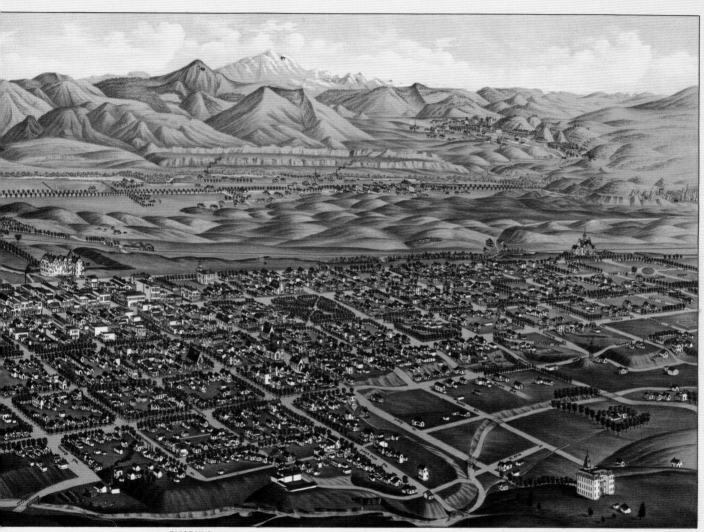

Beck & Pauli, Lithographers, Milwaukee, Wis.

PANORAMIC
BIRD'S EYE VIEW OF
COLORADO SPRINGS,
COLORADO CITY, MANITOU, COLO.

POPULATION 7,000   **1882.**   ALTITUDE 5975

Copyright 1882 by J. J. Stoner, Madison, Wis.

43. Depot D. & R. G. R. W.
44. School House.
45. Congregational Church.
46. Garden of the Gods.
47 Pike's Peak, 14,336 feet high.
48 Cameron's Cone.

23. Plaster Mill, Colorado City.
24. Brewery, Colorado City.
25. Colorado City School House.
26. Hotel.

HOTELS.
27. Palmer House.
28. Spaulding House, T. A. Himebaugh, Prop'r.
29. National Hotel.
30. Colorado Springs Hotel.
31. Crawford House.
32. Empire House, T. Jones, Prop'r.
33. Maxwell House, T. Maxwell, Prop'r.

34. Post Office.
35. Daily Gazette.
36. Daily Republican.
37. I. O. of O. F. Hall.
38. Masonic Hall, Opera House Building.

Manitou, Site of the Famous Soda and Iron Springs.
Altitude, 6,500 feet.
Principal Hotels.

39. Manitou House.
40. Beebee House.
41. Barker House, C. W. Barker, Prop'r.
42. Cliff House.

Fort Collins, Colorado (1899).
Fort Collins' growth can be seen in this map spanning thirty-four years of development from Merritt Dana Houghton's previous perspective map of the sparsely populated military outpost. Colorado Agricultural College (which later became Colorado State University) opened its doors in Fort Collins in 1879. Twenty years later, in 1899, Fort Collins had a population of about three thousand, with agriculture nourishing its economy as it grew into a prosperous Front Range town nestled against the foothills of the Rocky Mountains. Unlike many other bird's-eye views of the era, this map lacks the boastful vignettes of impressive buildings that signaled a city's pretensions to greatness. Fort Collins' success was of a more quiet, bucolic nature than that of cities such as Denver and Pueblo that grew to prominence based on their industrial might. This map, though understated compared to bird's-eye views of other Colorado cities, makes clear the development Fort Collins had achieved to this point, and the town's future promise is evident in the harmonious streets filled with homes and churches and in the rich farmland sprawling at its fringes.

PIKES PEAK

Pikes Peak panorama (1890).
Colorado Springs' proximity to the Rocky Mountains, which made the city a fashionable summer resort, is effectively displayed in this map, which seems more a painting of paradise than a map dedicated to conveying the facts of topography. Nineteenth-century advancements in printmaking allowed bird's-eye views to proliferate, creating relatively inexpensive and highly effective tools of town promotion. Maps such as this one allowed boosters to carefully craft a town's image and shape its identity: General Palmer's idyllic vision of the town he

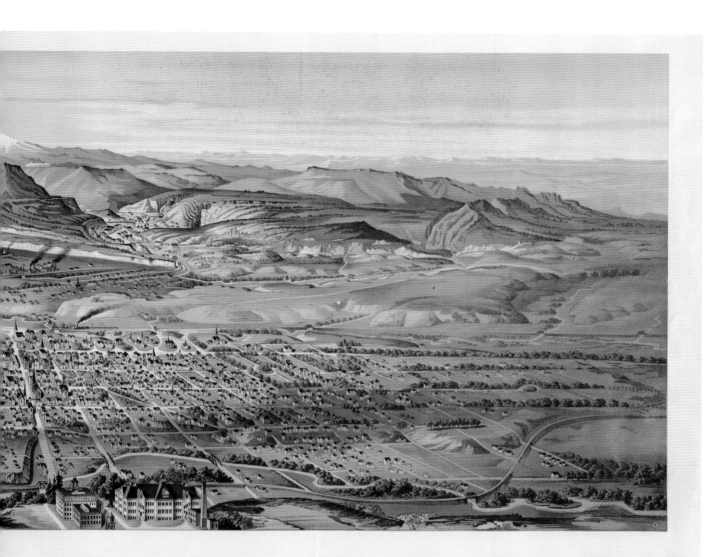

PANORAMA.

founded is made manifest in this map. The map artist has taken great care to create details such as the other-worldly rock formations of Garden of the Gods, the Pikes Peak cog railroad, which couldn't actually be seen with the naked eye from the map's perspective, and shadows cast by clouds in the foreground, which add an element of veracity to the scene.

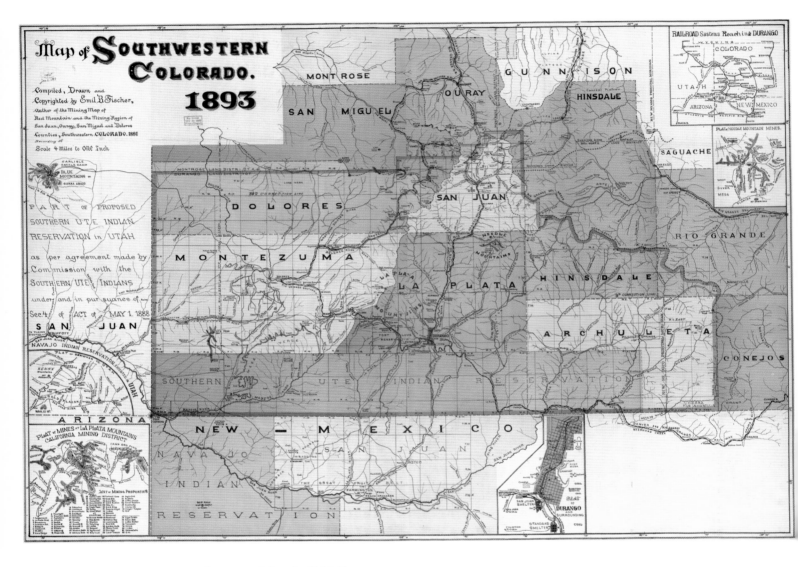

Map of Southwestern Colorado (1893).

As soon as the Utes, who had occupied the western area of what is now Colorado for centuries, ceded the San Juan Mountains in 1873, miners poured into the area. When they discovered precious metals, they quickly founded towns such as Silverton, Ouray, and Telluride, and they created new counties organized around the mining boomtowns. Durango, founded as a rail hub, emerged as the main smelting center and industrial city of the San Juan region and has remained the most important urban center for southwestern Colorado. This map was created by Emil Fischer, a Silverton-based artist and mapmaker who produced numerous hand-drawn, detailed depictions of the bustling San Juan region.

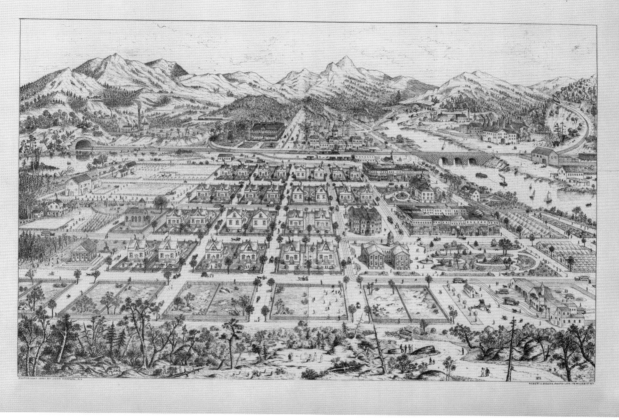

MAP
OF
GREAT WESTERN CENTRAL CITY.

Map of great western Central City. Robert A. Welcke, photo-lith (1887).

This map shows a town that does not exist and never did exist—other than in the imaginations of town planners, who in the heady times after the railroads arrived in Colorado seemed to build instant cities from scratch overnight and market them as potential economic powerhouses or mountain utopias. Industry, garden plots, and homes peacefully coexist in the tidy town portrayed on this map. Though not of an actual place, the map provides insight into the optimistic belief, prevalent in Victorian-era Colorado and evident in the perspective maps popular at the time, that western towns could be perfect places. These maps were instrumental in allaying the fears of easterners considering a move to the West. Instead of the brutal, lawless towns they had conjured in their imaginations, refined and gentle easterners saw in bird's-eye views a western paradise. Of course, neither imaginary image was entirely correct, and the truth lay somewhere in the middle.

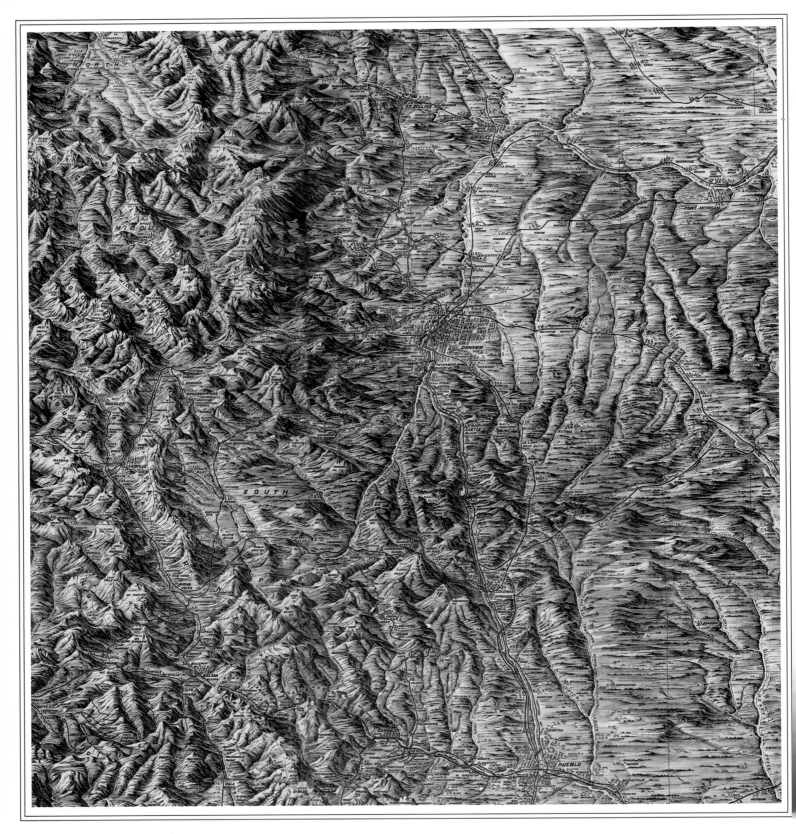

Detail of map on pages 98 and 99

Boom and Bust

Silver, though discovered in Colorado in the 1860s, had been overshadowed by gold. Low prices for the metal led to a lack of interest in mining it, but in 1878 Congress authorized the U.S. government to make large-scale silver purchases, and the race was on to find large lodes. The discovery of a rich silver deposit near Leadville in 1879 triggered a silver boom. Twenty years after the Pikes Peak Gold Rush, the Colorado Silver Boom was the second great mining boom in the state, and like the gold rush before it, the superheated period of mining activity led to a dramatic increase in Colorado's wealth and population, especially in mountain towns located near silver deposits. Leadville became one of the world's greatest mining camps and swiftly grew into a city, and several other towns in the surrounding area, such as Aspen, boomed when rich silver deposits were discovered.

As the nation's economy headed toward the chaos of the 1893 depression, however, the federal government dropped a bombshell on Colorado: It announced that it would stop purchasing silver. The bottom immediately fell out of the market. The price of silver sank so low that mines and smelters, unable to operate at a profit, shut down, putting an abrupt end to Colorado's silver bonanza and throwing thousands out of work. The Silver Panic swept the entire nation, but it hit Colorado particularly hard. Entire towns emptied as tens of thousands of out-of-work miners drifted down from the mountains and into Denver, seeking jobs. Hungry families begged in the streets, and makeshift towns sprang up in Denver to house the homeless masses. Crimes and suicides were rampant among the state's desperate citizens.

While Colorado's economy stagnated in the doldrums caused by the Silver Panic and civic leaders scrambled to find new ways to broaden the state's financial base beyond mining, a rancher and amateur prospector named Bob Womack spent his spare time looking at rocks in a place called Poverty Gulch. When he found gold, word spread among the state's desperate masses; soon Poverty Gulch was crawling with prospectors, and gold seekers crammed the Cripple Creek region surrounding Womack's find. Cripple Creek swelled into a small city with paved streets and electric lights, two opera houses, seventy-five saloons, eight newspapers, and its own stock exchange. Over the next few years, the Cripple Creek Mining District became the biggest bonanza in Colorado's history and the richest gold camp in the United States.

Realizing that every boom is followed by a bust, state leaders used wealth from the gold mines to diversify Colorado's economy, a process that had begun in the wake of the silver bust. Reservoirs were constructed to improve irrigation, and what was once considered wasteland was repackaged by Colorado boosters as a lush and bountiful Eden. Agriculture eclipsed mining as the state's most profitable industry. Cattle ranching was encouraged on the plains, and in the mountain parks and valleys, ranchers raised alfalfa to winter-feed their stock. Cowboys flocked to Colorado, giving rise to rodeos, such as the world-famous National Western Stock Show. Manufacturers were given incentives to set up shop in Colorado, and advertising campaigns targeting tourists proclaimed Colorado a vacation paradise with a plentitude of pretty countryside and dramatic mountain vistas. The state's sanatoriums for tuberculosis sufferers were touted, and sufferers with sick lungs and healthy bank accounts were encouraged to seek the cure in Colorado amid its dry air and ample sunshine. Tuberculosis ultimately brought far more newcomers to Colorado than the arrival of the railroads or the mining booms ever had.

The Cripple Creek Gold Rush proved to be the greatest precious-metal mining bonanza in the state's history—and its last. After the gold played out at Cripple Creek, the Colorado economy had many more ups and downs caused by boom-and-bust cycles as it gobbled up everything from oil shale to uranium. The state had to rely on other resources, such as its comfortable climate and its bounty of mountain snow, to provide it with steady sustenance.

POPULATION 16,000
BIRD'S EYE VIEW OF

LEADVILLE, COLO.
1882.

Copyright 1882 by J. J. Stoner, Madison, Wis.

Published by J. J. Stoner, Madison, Wis.

1. Court House.
2. Post Office.
3. Tabor Opera House.
4. Central School.
5. Ninth St. School.
6. Seventh St. School.
7. Carbonate Hill School.
8. Central Fire Station.
9. Hose House No. 3.
10. Harrison Reduction Works branch of St. Louis Smelting and Refining Co., St. Louis, Franz Fohr, General Manager.
11. A. R. Meyers, Sampling Co.'s, Works, Chas. T. Limberg, General Manager.
12. Elgin Smelting Works.
13. Cummings & Finn, Smelting Works.

15. Foundry, Boiler and Machine Works, Farrow & Co., Prop's.
16. Excelsior Iron Works, Foundry and Machine Shop, A. Falkenau, Prop.
17. Pacific Iron Works, Foundry and Machine Shop, Frank Guy, Prop.
18. Brewery, Henry W. Gaw, Prop.
19. Franklin House, Jos. Becker, Prop.
20. Fifth Ave. Hotel, A. H. Kellogg, Prop.
21. Grand Pacific Hotel, Wm. A. Keller, Prop.
22. Maine House, C. F. Daly, Prop.
23. Bank of Leadville.
24. City Bank.
25. First National Bank.
26. Merchants and Mechanics Bank.

27. Gas Works.
29. Denver and Rio Grande R. R. Depot.
30. Denver and Rio Grande R. R. Round House.
31. Boor and Sash Warehouse and Lumber Yard.
J. D. Griffiths, Prop.
32. Planing Mill and Shingle Manuf'y, W. D. Scott, Prop.
33. Tabor Milling Company's Works.
33. The Leadville Daily and Weekly Democrat, Democrat Printing Co., Publishers.
34. The Leadville Daily and Weekly Herald, Herald Printing Co., Publishers.

35. Chronicle.
36. Leadville Gold and Silver Mill Co.
A—Baptist Church.
B—Congregational Church.
C—Episcopal "
D—Methodist "
E—Presbyterian "
F—Roman Catholic Church of Annunciation.
G—"   "   " of Sacred Heart.
H—A. Methodist Episcopal Church.
K—St. Vincent Hospital.

Bird's eye view of Leadville, Colo. H. Wellge, del. Beck & Pauli, lithographers (1882).
Finely rendered details such as puffy clouds, timbered hills, and plumes of smoke flagging in the wind above factories lend bird's-eye-view maps such as this one an air of artistry. People walking around town and riding in horse-drawn carriages, a train moving along tracks, and boats sailing on a lake give this map a sense of movement and vibrant life absent in the sterile cartography of maps designed solely to convey the spatial relationships between areas and objects. Leadville during the heyday of the Colorado Silver Boom is depicted here. The civic pride behind this map, and its creators' intention of fostering more commercial growth, are evident in the details both of the mining operations in the area and of the cultural amenities, such as schools, opera houses, newspaper offices, and churches, that were financed by mining profits as Leadville expanded into a mountain metropolis.

Published by J. J. Stoner, Madison. Wis.

1. School House.
2. Post Office, George A. Haynes, Post Master.
3. D. &. R. G. R. R. Depot.
4. Knights of Pythias Hall.
5. Colorado Mining Ledger, Dr. J. H. Nonemaker,
    Editor and Prop'r.

BIRD'S E

MAYSVI

CHAFF

1

Copyright 1882 by

Bird's eye view of Maysville, Colo. Chaffee County 1882. Beck & Pauli, lithographers (1882).
Maysville was a substantial silver mining town served by the Denver and Rio Grande Railroad. Originally
founded as "Feather Ranch," it combined with a nearby tent camp called "Crazy Creek" to become, by 1882, Chaffee County's largest town. Maysville boasted dance halls, several hotels, a bank, a post office, two newspapers,

EW OF

E , COLO.

OUNTY

2.

er, Madison, Wis.

Beck & Paul, Lithographers, Milwaukee, Wis.

A—Congregational Church.
B—Union Sunday School Building.
C—Venable House, Mrs. J. I. Venable, Proprietress.
D—Hughes House, Mike Doyle, Prop'r.
E—Erie Smelting Works, G. W. Jones, Supt.

well-stocked stores, and a half dozen saloons before the Silver Panic of 1893 put an end to the party and turned Maysville to a ghost town. Today only a restored schoolhouse remains of the once-bustling Maysville. Though many of the Colorado towns depicted in bird's-eye views continued to thrive, some fell into decline and became sorry remnants of their glory days that were depicted in panoramic maps. Some vanished entirely.

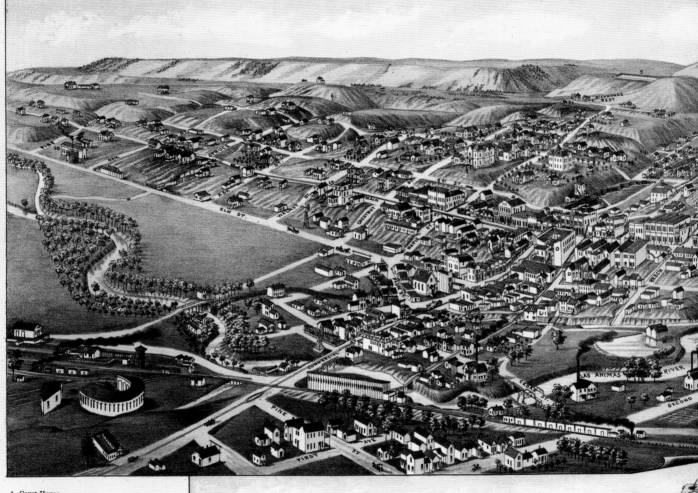

1. Court House.
2. School House.
3. Post Office.
4. Water Works.
5. Reservoir.
6. A. T. & S. F. R. R. Depot.
7. A. T. & S. F. Round House.
8. Jaffa's Opera House.
9. Mitchell's Hall.
10. Gas Works.
12. Saddler&Harrness M'f'y, F. Burkhard & Co., Prop's.
13. Rocky Mountain Flour Mill, Barnes Bros., Prop's.
14. Trinidad City Mill, Jose A. Salazor, Prop.
15. Planing Mill, F. H. Keith, Prop.

Published by J. J. Stoner, Madison, Wis.

16. Planing Mill, Door and Sash Factory, Leedham & Son, Prop.
17. Rocky Mountain Planing Mill, Door and Sash Factory, Phillips & Cummings, Prop's.

NORTH SIDE.

TRINIDAD, COLO.

1882.

COUNTY SEAT OF LAS ANIMAS COUNTY

Population 3500.

Rifenburg
Raton Pe
Trinidad,
Simpson's

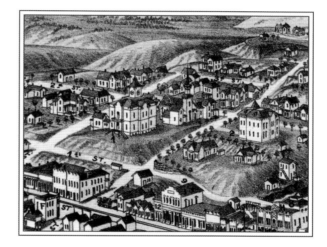

Trinidad, Colo. 1882 county seat of Las Animas County.
Beck & Pauli, lithographers.

Created by prolific panoramic-map artist J. J. Stoner, this map depicts the town of Trinidad, located at the heart of Colorado's extensive southern coalfield. Trinidad boomed because of nearby coal mines and became one of Colorado's biggest and richest cities. When labor disputes between miners and the coal companies in nearby Ludlow led to a strike, strike-related violence escalated, eventually culminating in the 1914 Ludlow Massacre, in which the Colorado National Guard attacked a tent camp of coal miners, killing twenty people. The Ludlow violence is considered one of the deadliest labor wars in American history.

X—Masonic and Odd Fellows Hall.
A—Methodist Episcopal Church.
B—Methodist Episcopal South Church.
C—Presbyterian Church.
D—Roman Catholic Church.
E—Roman Catholic Convent.
F—Bank of Southern Colorado, S. T. Collins, Cashier.
G—First National Bank.
H—Trinidad Daily News, Olney Newell, Editor and Prop.
K—Trinidad Democrat, H. K. Cutting, Editor and Prop.
L—Brewery, Henry Schneider, Prop.
M—Baker House, Geo. W. Baker, Prop.
N—Trinidad Hotel, Olof Ross, Prop.
O—Grand Union Hotel.
P—United States Hotel

x Pauli, Lithographers, Milwaukee, Wis.

2½ Miles out.
above level of the sea.
"   "   "   "
feet above level of the sea.

Perspective map of the city of Denver, Colo. H. Wellge, des. (1889).

Denver is booming at this point, but there are still many platted areas at the edges of the city available for development, and Denver has yet to start its epic sprawl across the prairie. Displayed here in finely detailed insets are some of Denver's most beautiful buildings that are still standing, such as Trinity Church, and other buildings that have fallen to the wrecking ball as the city reinvented itself, such as the Tabor Opera House. The Colorado State Capitol Building is part of the cityscape in this map, though its construction had only just begun at the time the map was made. Glaringly absent in this and every map of Denver is a navigable waterway. Most U.S. cities featured in panoramic maps were situated along a major river, a lake, or an ocean: Access to waterways was a crucial element of the infrastructure that allowed viable urban areas to develop in America. Denver's South Platte River was too shallow to support boat traffic; thus landlocked Denver, without access to a waterway allowing the shipment of mail and supplies, was entirely dependent in its early years upon railroads to link it to the nation's economy. Along the South Platte River, smelters, which by the time of this map's production had become Denver's largest industry, belch plumes of black smoke. A pastoral mountain panorama with Pikes Peak and Grays Peak is featured (Grays Peak is misnamed on this map—it cannot be seen from the city because it is shielded by the Mount Evans massif). The mountains to the west of Denver are depicted here as part of a friendly looking parkland—a far cry from the howling wilderness that challenged early explorers and prospectors and often claimed their lives. Denver, fully settled and enjoying the fruits of economic prosperity, is beginning to view the mountains as objects of beauty and places of solace offering refuge from the frenetic cityscape on the plains below.

COPYRIGHTED AND PUBLISHED BY AMERICAN PUBLISHING CO. 205 SECOND STR. MILWAUKEE WIS.

PERSPECTIVE MAP OF THE CITY OF

DENVER, COLO.

1889.

THE CITY HAS 85 CHURCHES, 17 BANKS, 18 RAILROADS AND 44 NEWSPAPERS.

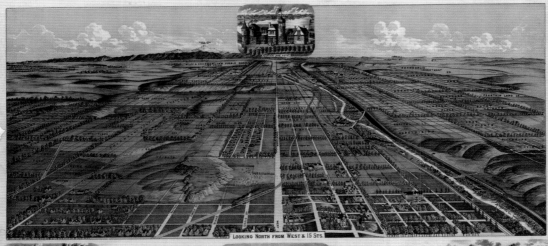

LOOKING NORTH FROM WEST & 15 STS.

COPYRIGHTED AND PUBLISHED BY AMERICAN PUBLISHING CO COR SOUTH WATER & FERRY STS, MILWAUKEE WIS

LOOKING SOUTH FROM WEST & 15 STS.

PUEBLO, COLO.

1890
POPULATION 30,000

REAL ESTATE, LOANS AND INVESTMENTS.

National Land & Improvement Co., Geo. H. Paisons, Manager, 424 Santa Fe Ave.
North Pueblo Land & Improvement Co., Chas. W. Prisney, Agent, Cor. Max & Jones Ave.
Colorado Coal & Iron Co., Geo. H. Lyman & Co., Land Agents, Main office cor. B. and Victoria Streets.
G. L. Wiley & Co., Agents for Chamberlin Invest. Co. 227 Santa Fe Avenue.
Hunt & McClees, Office 718, Santa Fe Ave.
Williams & Nullolly, Office, cor. South Union and B. Streets.

H. S. Van Krohn & Co., Office, 724 Santa Fe Avenue.
Tittes, Telfues & Co., Office, 114 W. Second Street.
H. D. Misy & Co., 243 North Union Street.
Huston & Bruner, 203 South Union Street.
W. H. Harvey, 718 Santa Fe Avenue.
D. L. Holden & Co., 222 North Union St.
Kern, Greene & Daniels, 227 South Union Street.
E. G. Martz & Co., 280 South Union St.
Norris & Dreillie, 402 Santa Fe Avenue.
L. H. Roberts, Southern Hotel.
Holland & Miles, W. C & S. Union Streets.
Hogan & Koyel South Union Avenue.

Olney & Hill, cor. Main and Union Streets.
Rosenbild Construction Co., cor. Westward Main Streets.
H. P. Murphee & Co., 220 Santa Fe Ave.
Chas. A. Sanceford, 724 Santa Fe Avenue.
I. S. Merrill, 714 Santa Fe Avenue.
Scott & Stillings, 414 Santa Fe Avenue.
Swun & Ashfelts, 214 West Second Street.
Dowsen Gibson, Investment Co., 402 Santa Fe Avenue.
Bernsholler & Wells, W. 15th and Santa Fe Avenues.
C. H. Small & Co., 230 Santa Fe Avenue.
J. L. Scott & Son, 728 Santa Fe Avenue.

BANKS & BANKERS.

First National Bank, cor. Fourth and Santa Fe.
Central National Bank, cor. C. and South Union.
Bank of Pueblo, cor. Fourth and Santa Fe.
Western National Bank, cor C. and South Union.
American National Bank, cor. Fourth and North Union.
Chas. D. Hinkley & Co., 228 South Union.
Stock Growers National Bank, cor. Third and Santa Fe.
Benshimer State, 412 Santa Fe.

MANUFACTURING AND COMMERCIAL.

Cooley & Roof, Manufacturers of Crackers and Confectionery, W. Fourth Street.
Pueblo Foundry and Machine Shops South Santa Fe Avenue.
J. W. Swarren, Attorney at Law, cor. Sixth and Santa Fe.
Murry & Coms, Attorneys at Law, 421 Santa Fe.
Samuel C. Spencer, Attorney at Law, 200 Santa Fe.
G. L. Walt, Books and Stationery.
Stansfield & Bro., Pueblo Steam Laundry, 200 Santa Fe and South Union Avenues.
L. L. Gates & Co., Clothing 221 Santa Fe.
P. S. Sutherland, Dentist, Swift Block, cor. Sixth and Main.

WHOLESALE GROCERS.

Anderson Bros., 122 to 128 Santa Fe.
Dinbrough & Joy, 126 to 132 Front Street.
Chas. H. Hitchel & Co., 402 Main Street.
Gamble & Co., Retail Grocers. 223 Santa Fe Avenue.

HOTELS.

Grand Hotel, cor. Eighth and Santa Fe.
St. James Hotel, cor. Fifth and Santa Fe.
Southern Hotel, B. and Victoria.
Fancho Hotel, 126 to 202 N. Union.
Fountain Lake Hotel, Fountain Lake.

Henry, G. Martin, Insurance, 206 Santa Fe.
Knight & Lewis, Insurance, 220 S. Union.
W. M. Groups, Photographer, 222 Santa Fe Avenue.
J. W. Shaw, Photographer, 125 W. Fourth Street.

Pueblo, Colo. (1890).

After steel made from Colorado coal and iron ore was first manufactured in Pueblo in the early 1880s, for a time Pueblo developed into the second-largest city in the state, and it established itself as the most important industrial center in southern Colorado, earning it the nickname "Pittsburgh of the West." The plumes of smoke coming from the smelting works on this map signal Pueblo's prosperity. Billowing smoke, instead of being seen as harmful pollution, was viewed by Coloradans during the early industrial era as a sign of progress and a potent symbol of a city's wealth. Smoke from smelters and steelworks smelled like money.

Bird's eye view of Aspen, Pitkin Co., Colo. (1893).

More than fifty years before the ski lifts arrived and Aspen became
famous for its snowy slopes, its mountains produced riches of the
silver sort. In the late 1880s Aspen replaced Leadville as Colorado's
leading silver city. As depicted on this map, boomtown Aspen
boasted a public tramway system and a wealth of new buildings,
including smelters, schools, theaters, and banks. When paper
became scarce during a blizzard, the *Aspen Times* printed its daily
edition on the only paper available: old copies of this map stock-
piled in its office. A story on the front of the one-page newspaper
explained why there was a map on the back. In silver-boom Aspen,
necessity was the mother of recycling.

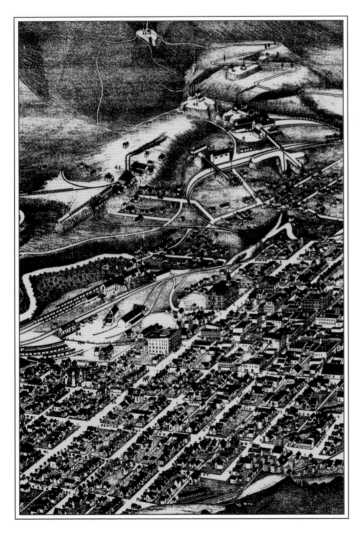

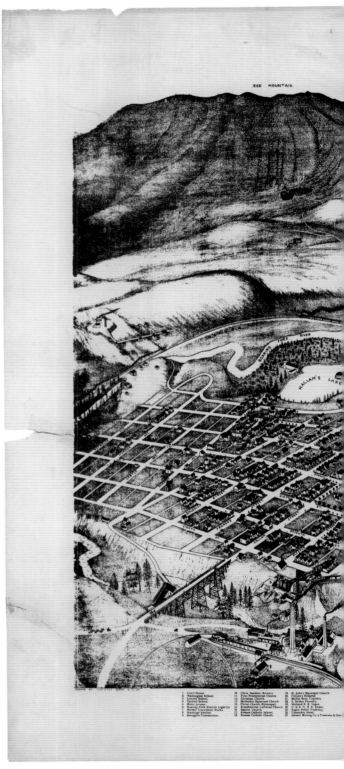

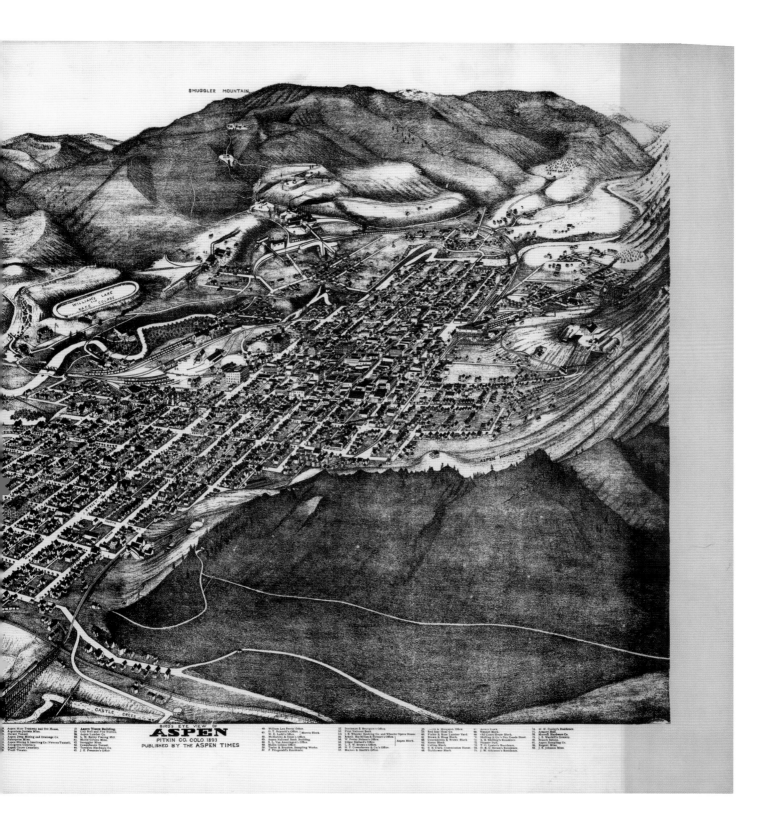

BIRD'S EYE VIEW OF
ASPEN
PITKIN CO. COLO. 1893
PUBLISHED BY THE ASPEN TIMES

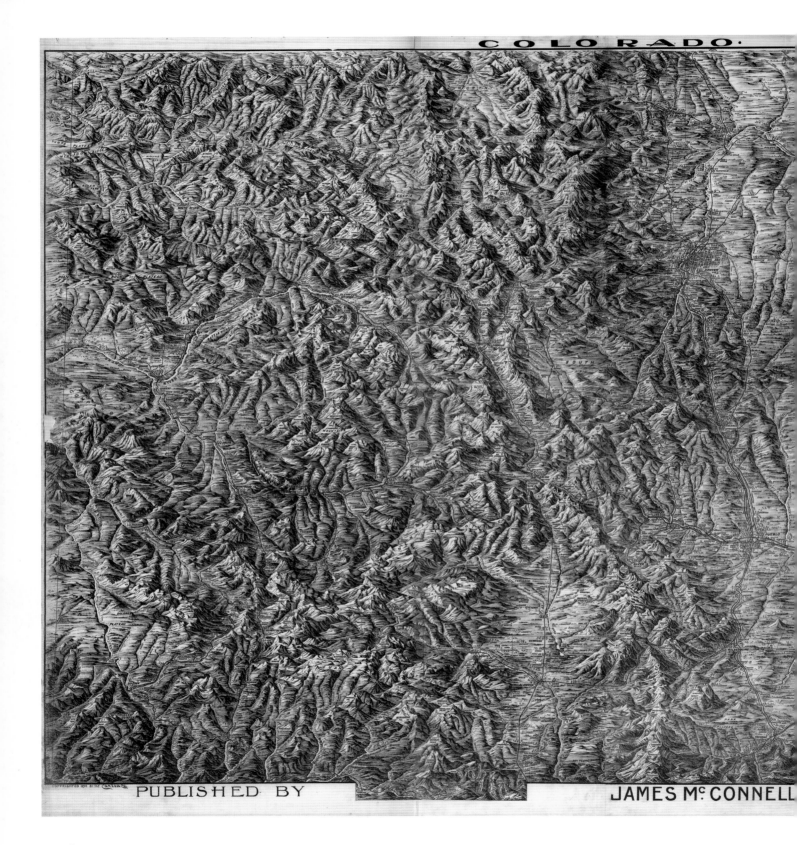

PUBLISHED BY

JAMES MᶜCONNELL

Colorado / Caxton Co.; drawn & lith. by F. Pezolt (1894).
This map, created by James McConnell School Supplies of Denver, uses artfully rendered shaded relief to depict Colorado's mountains. It is dense with detail (see page 84) and shows at least two hundred towns that no longer exist in the state—many of them victims of mining busts in the mountains, many of them abandoned during droughts on the eastern plains, many of them killed by the rise of the automobile culture. In the time before automobiles, the state needed tiny towns in every settled area to provide people with food and supplies; as roads and private cars became more widely available, many of these small towns became unnecessary and faded into obscurity. Original McConnell maps that measure roughly four feet by six feet are sometimes rescued from old schoolhouses that are collapsing or being torn down and then make their way into public archives or private collections. These enormous roll maps, glued to a linen canvas backer and designed to scroll down over a school chalkboard, once provided Colorado's children an opportunity to study the state's mining camps, towns, rivers, and mountains; they now provide map aficionados and historians a fascinating window into Colorado's past.

COMPLIMENTS OF THE
GRIPPLE CREEK
SUNDAY HERALD.
SOUVENIR EDITION, 1896.

CRIPPLE CREEK MINING DISTRICT.
THE GREAT GOLD CAMP OF COLORADO.

BIRD'S EYE VIEW
C. H. AMBRINE,
CRIPPLE CREEK.

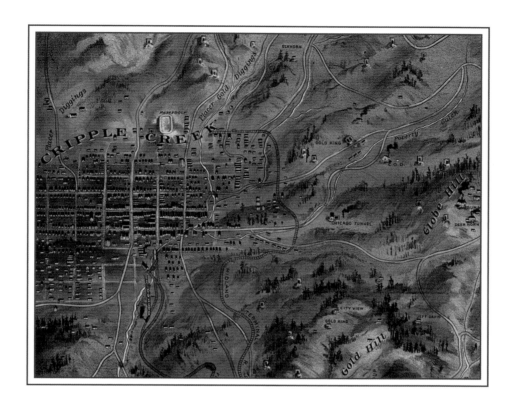

Cripple Creek mining district, the great gold camp of Colorado / bird's eye view by C. H. Amerine; compliments of the **Cripple Creek Sunday Herald** *(1895).*

This aerial view illustrates how the Cripple Creek Mining District's towns filled small valleys amid a vast expanse of mountains and were linked by serpentine railways to nearby mines perched amid rugged terrain. Pikes Peak, which became both reference point and symbol for the prospectors racing to join the first Colorado gold rush, appears on this map of Colorado's new gold rush towns as a bright, snowy landmark in the distance. At the time this map was made, the Wright brothers' airplane was eight years away from leaving the earth and flight was still a dream. Mapmakers had to study details on the ground and then guess at how they would look from above. Their intimate knowledge of the land they studied firsthand led to map creations depicting the texture of the terrain in a way that, while not as technically accurate as the topographical maps of the next century, feels very real and connects viscerally with the viewer. The challenges of traveling through Colorado's mountains and settling among them are perhaps more vividly portrayed in a panoramic map such as this one than in a map that hasn't been touched by an artist's brush and whose mountains are girded with contour lines to merely suggest their ruggedness and majesty.

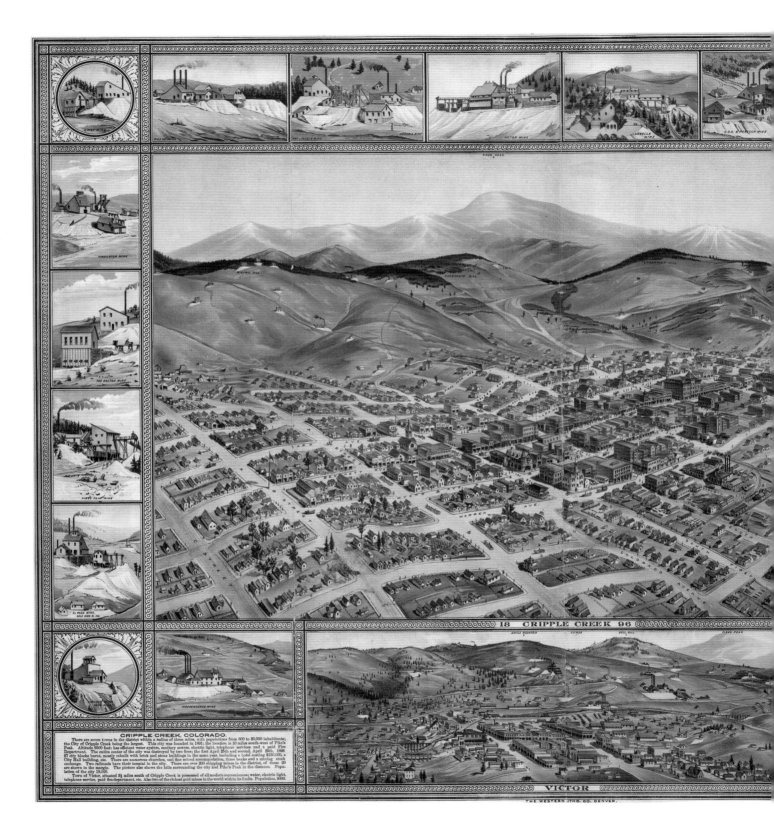

CRIPPLE CREEK, COLORADO.

There are seven towns in the district within a radius of three miles, with populations from 600 to 20,000 inhabitants; the City of Cripple Creek being the largest. This city was founded in 1891; the location is 10 miles south-west of Pike's Peak. Altitude 9500 feet; has efficient water system, sanitary sewers, electric light, telephone services and a paid Fire Department. The entire center of the city was destroyed by two fires; the first April 25th and second, April 29th, 1896; 27 city blocks burnt, mostly rebuilt with brick and stone buildings in the same year, including a hotel costing $150,000, a City Hall building, etc. There are numerous churches, and fine school accommodation, three banks and a mining stock exchange. Two railroads have their terminal in the city. There are over 300 shipping mines in the district, of these 20 are shown in the margin. The picture also shows the hills surrounding the city and Pike's Peak in the distance. Population of the city 19,000.

Town of Victor, situated 5½ miles south of Cripple Creek is possessed of all modern conveniences; water, electric light, telephone service, paid fire department, etc. Also two of the richest gold mines in the world within its limits. Population, 9000.

Cripple Creek (1896).

This gorgeous panoramic map features Cripple Creek and the mines that created the greatest gold boom in Colorado's history. Cripple Creek burned to the ground in 1896, and buildings formerly made of wood were reconstructed with brick; the newly rebuilt town is shown in this map. Though this map was mass produced by lithography, which uses a chemical process to create an image and doesn't require the same level of craftsmanship that hand engraving and hand coloring demand, the images were drawn by an artisan who paid careful attention to detail. Printing technology changed dramatically throughout the nineteenth century: By the time this map was made, efficient high-volume production had replaced slow, labor-intensive techniques. Many maps, however, were still being created not simply as utilitarian devices to convey information but as beautiful objects, whose originals today fetch high prices with collectors and whose reproductions are popular adornments of contemporary homes and businesses throughout Colorado. Scholars for many years disdained bird's-eye views because of their commercial overtones and their creators' penchant for whimsical embellishment, but the bird's-eye-view-map genre is now regarded as providing important insight into urban geography, city planning, and the history of architecture in Colorado's cities and towns.

ANCHORIA LELAND MINE

Bird's eye view of Denver, Colorado,.
Denver Lith. Co. (1908).

The year this map was produced, 1908, is significant for being the first time the Democratic National Convention was held in Denver; it was also the year that the Colorado State Capitol Building's dome was plated with genuine gold to commemorate the city's gold-rush roots. This attractive map captures the vitality of Colorado's main urban center by depicting Denver in a golden era of development. At this point Denver has weathered the Silver Panic of 1893 and is enjoying the rich rewards of Cripple Creek, one of the greatest bonanzas in mining history. An index of Denver's many thriving businesses is provided, vibrant urban street scenes and iconic buildings such as the Brown Palace Hotel are featured in the photo insets, and the Denver Auditorium, completed in time to host the Democratic National Convention, is on prominent display in a vignette at the bottom center of the map. The nightmarish traffic patterns that downtown Denver endures to this day are in large part the product of a confusing grid of streets that were at first laid parallel to the south bank of Cherry Creek near its confluence with the South Platte River, with perpendicular cross streets. But as Denver spilled across its original boundaries, streets were arranged in a north-south and east-west orientation. The strangely intersecting streets that resulted are evident in this map. At the time of this map's production, Colorado was on the cusp of being transformed by cars, and the Colburn Roadster, built in Denver by the Colburn Automobile Company, is highlighted in a vignette at the top of the map. When private automobiles became all the rage, out-of-town competition from such auto giants as Ford Motor Company shut down Colburn and other local auto manufacturers. Streets were smoothly paved to make way for the new mode of transportation that replaced train travel, radically transforming the landscape, culture, and economy of Colorado. Denver's ample parks are also depicted in this map: Though Mayor Robert Speer's political career was highly controversial, he succeeded through a City Beautiful campaign in physically remaking Denver into an attractive city filled with parkways and greenbelts, a process that began shortly before this map was made and left a legacy that has endured to this day.

BIRD'S EYE VIEW OF
DENVER, COLORADO, 1908
Looking South from Twenty-Third Street Viaduct.

DENVER AUDITORIUM · SEATING CAPACITY 12000

Birdseye View from South Broadway ... Showing

HARLEM, JACKSONS BROADWAY HEIGHTS & CITY OF DENVER

A.F. HARASZTHY   WITH   W.J. VOIT
Colorado Land Headquarters
814-17TH ST. DENVER, COLO.   PHONE MAIN 8389

COPYRIGHT 1906. BY A.F. HARASZTHY & W.J. VOIT

A.E. MITCHELL — DENVER ENGRAVING CO.

LOTS FOR SALE
An Improved Lot in HARLEM or a Lot in JACKSON'S BROADWAY HEIGHTS for $5 a Month.

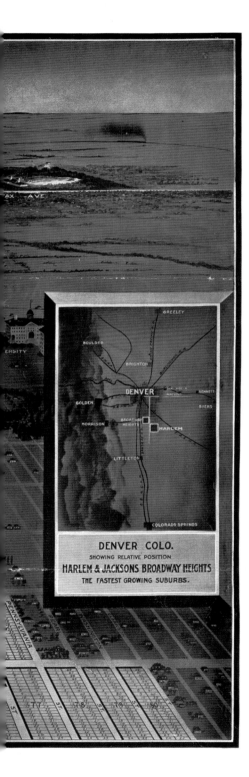

Birdseye view from South Broadway . . . showing Harlem, Jacksons Broadway Heights & city of Denver. [Signed:] A. E. Mitchell. Denver Engraving Co. A. F. Haraszthy, W. J. Voit with Colorado Land Headquarters (1907).

As Denver grew, real estate prices rose, and the city spread across the plains, giving rise to bedroom communities, such as the ones plotted on this map, looking from south of the city toward the north and advertising "the fastest growing suburbs." Communities such as these were originally connected to the city center by streetcars. But public transportation gave way to private automobiles as roads and suburban sprawl filled in many of the state's open places, and Colorado faced a new challenge: how to manage the consequences of the growth it had so desperately sought for so long.

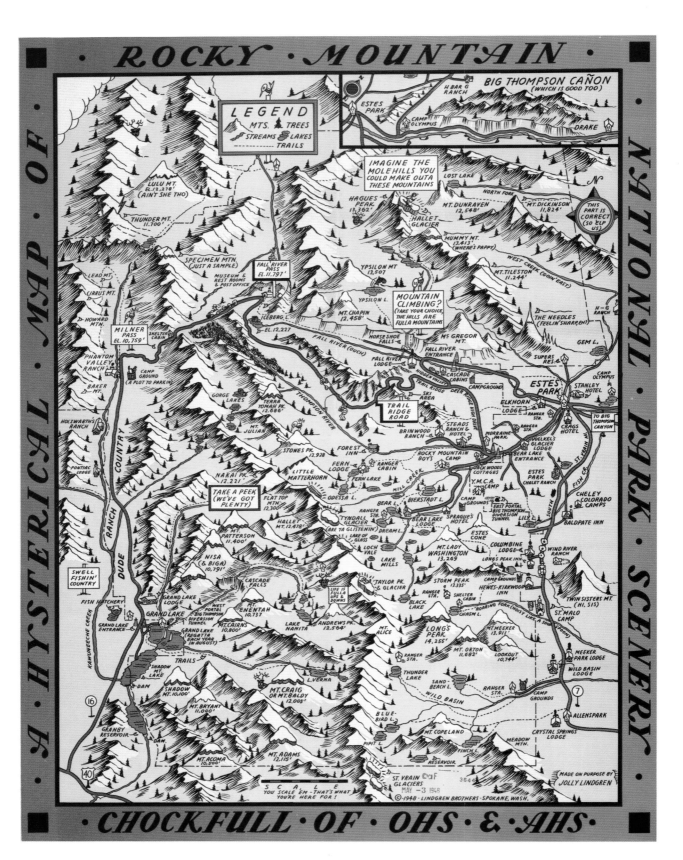

Natural Resource Management

As Colorado's population expanded, accommodating all the new arrivals caused massive changes to the land. Open prairie was cut by steel tracks and rows of power lines. The automobile age arrived, bringing with it endless miles of pavement. Enormous concrete reservoirs and canal systems were constructed to store and divert the precious resource of water. The Uncompahgre Valley project, an irrigation tunnel connecting the Gunnison River with the watershed of the Uncompahgre River, was the nation's first large-scale diversion of water from the drainage system of one river to another. The Colorado–Big Thompson project, started in the 1930s, grew into a byzantine system of dams, dikes, reservoirs, tunnels, and power plants designed to transport water across the Continental Divide from the water-rich Western Slope of the Rockies to the dry and heavily populated Eastern Slope. Because of these and dozens of other massive water projects, agriculture became more important to the Colorado economy than mining, and population centers in arid areas expanded unrestrained by lack of water. Upon land once deemed uninhabitable desert, Colorado's urban core began morphing into a 175-mile-long megalopolis of Front Range cities, with Denver at its center and the satellites of Colorado Springs, Pueblo, Boulder, Greeley, and Fort Collins spreading at its edges, nudging their way into the mountain foothills and spilling across the plains.

Rocky Mtn National Park (1951).
The Colorado Rockies are portrayed in this "hysterical map" as a wilderness subdued: a place of safe, family fun, where cars roll along newly paved highways and tourists produce endless "ohs & ahs" while cracking corny jokes and viewing pretty scenery.

With development came consequences: dirty air and foul rivers, devastated forests, and diminished wildlife populations. Coloradans began to appreciate the land in its unadulterated state, and mountain ranges that had once seemed nothing more than nuisances to be tamed with tunnels and roads came to be valued for their scenery and recreational opportunities. Throughout the twentieth century, while Colorado was becoming densely developed, special landscapes were protected. Between 1902 and 1907 fourteen new forest reserves were established by President Theodore Roosevelt in Colorado, and older reserves were enlarged, creating a total of eighteen forests containing almost 16 million acres—about one-fifth of the state's land. After being combined and consolidated, the reserves were renamed "National Forests"; they became iconic features of the state's landscape integral both to conserving natural resources and to developing important Colorado enterprises such as cattle ranching, tourism, and skiing. In 1915, responding to passionate naturalist Enos Mills and other Colorado conservationists, Congress created Rocky Mountain National Park, 405 square miles of wilderness and mountain scenery that became a centerpiece of the Colorado tourism industry. In 1946 a Chicago industrialist, with the help of former members of the 10th Mountain Division who had trained for alpine combat in World War II at nearby Camp Hale, began

transforming the dilapidated mining town of Aspen into a world-class skiing and cultural resort. Ski resorts soon spread throughout the Colorado Rockies, giving birth to a lucrative industry and becoming a linchpin of the state's economy. The mountains that had once served as a barrier to exploration and a hindrance to settlement had become Colorado's most significant asset.

By the time the ski industry was born in Colorado, twentieth-century technology had allowed cartography to achieve levels of accuracy unimaginable in the nineteenth century. Bird's-eye views, with their attention to detail and artistic flourishes, vanished and were replaced by road maps depicting Colorado's network of highways, utilitarian maps of its urban centers, and U.S. Geological Survey (USGS) topographic maps of its landscape. Today contour lines based on data collected by the USGS indicate the staggering scale of Colorado's mountains. What is missing in the new breed of maps is the quirky human presence found in the classic maps of Colorado's past.

Bird's-eye views, while lacking the geographic correctness of modern maps, had a unique excellence all their own. They portrayed towns, and the people who lived in those towns, in relation to the state's land. Mountains were paintings of peaks with craggy shoulders and snowcapped summits, not abstract lines indicating elevation. In bird's-eye views carriages stuttered down dirt streets and trains proudly rolled along rails. Flags rippled in the wind, smoke curled out of chimneys, and shadows passed over the land. The maps were full of life; there was drama in their hand-drawn details. And they had a point of view: Not only did they look at a town from above and at a specific angle, but they were created with an agenda in mind—to make Colorado's boomtowns appear magnificent. Whether their per-spectives, cartographic or otherwise, were flawed hardly seems the point. Unlike the computer-generated, technically accurate but dishwater-dull maps so often produced today, with the maps of the nineteenth century, the human hand that created them was always visible, and imagination and crafts-manship were as important as facts. Those maps may have been wrong, but they were beautiful.

Detail of map on page 108

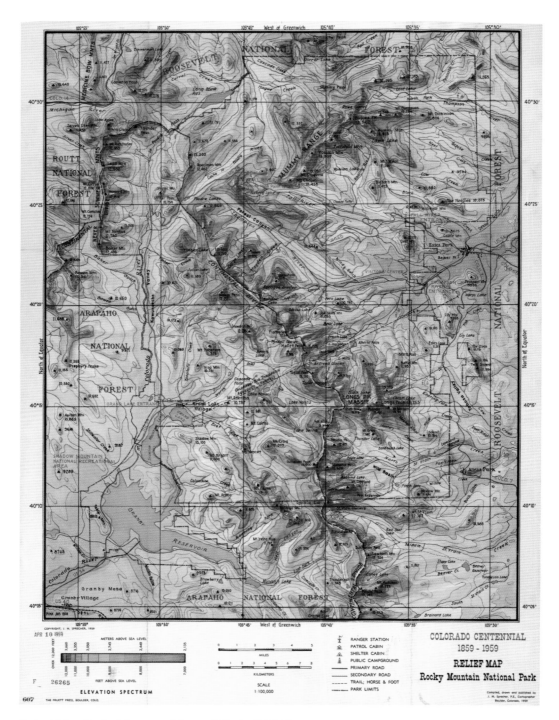

Relief Map Rocky Mountain National Park (1959).

This map uses contour lines and coloring to indicate elevation, rendering the great spine of the Continental Divide readily apparent. It was competently created, but the craftsmanship of earlier eras, from the exquisite scrollwork on the cartouches of maps made with hand-engraved copperplates to the hand-drawn details of bird's-eye views rich with the imagination of the artist who envisioned them, was becoming as old-fashioned as railroads. When the digital age dawned, maps as attractive as the mountains they depicted were encased in museum displays, and contour lines connecting data points charted a path toward the future.

Acknowledgments

The publisher and the authors gratefully acknowledge the staff at the Library of Congress for their fine work and research assistance on this book, particularly Aimee Hess, Ralph Eubanks, and Colleen Cahill.

Without the vision and professionalism of Erin Turner, this audacious project would not be the permanent achievement it is bound to be.

—Vincent Virga

I am grateful for the assistance of the hardworking and helpful staffs of the Denver Public Library, the Colorado Historical Society, the Rocky Mountain Map Society, the University of Colorado at Boulder Map Library, and the Library of Congress.

While researching this book, I benefited greatly from the generous guidance and advice of three of America's most knowledgeable map aficionados: Myron West, Wes Brown, and Curtis Bird. Their knowledge of cartography humbled me; their endless fascination with maps inspired me.

I would like to thank the book's editor, Erin Turner, for providing me with the opportunity to work on such a fascinating project and for her valuable input. Thanks also to Julie Marsh for her hard work fine-tuning the manuscript. Many thanks to Vincent Virga for his enthusiastic involvement with this project.

Completing this book would not have been possible for me without the support, encouragement and sage advice of my wife, Amy.

—Stephen Grace

All maps come from the Library of Congress Geography and Map Division unless otherwise noted. To order reproductions of Library of Congress items, please contact the Library of Congress Photoduplication Service, Washington, D.C. 20540-4570 or (202) 707-5640.

Page ii Detail from John Kohfahl, "Map of great western Central City. (Imaginary place)," Robert A. Welcke, photo-lith., New York, c1887. G9930 1887 .K6.

Page viii Ruysch, Johann. "Universalior cogniti orbis tabula." In Claudius Ptolemeus, *Geographia.* Rome, 1507. G1005.1507 Vault.

Page ix. Waldseemüller, Martin. "Universalis cosmographia secudum Ptholomaei traditionem et Americi Vespucii aloru[m] que lustrations," St. Dié, France?, 1507. G32001507.W3 Vault.

Pages 6–7 "Le Nouveau Mexique appele aussi nouvelle grenade et Marata. Avec Partie de Californie." 1742. G4420 1742 .C6 TIL.

Page 8 Carte Nouvelle de La Partie de L'Ouest de La Louisianne Bénard de La Harpe. Drawn: 1723–1725. Manuscript Division, Library of Congress.

Page 9 Sayer, Robert. "A new map of North America, with the British, French, Spanish, Dutch & Danish dominions on that great continent; and the West India Islands, done from the latest geographers, with great improvements from the Sieurs d'Anville & Robert." London, Printed for Robt. Sayer [1750?]. 1750 .S3 Vault.

Page 10 Smet, Pierre-Jean de. "[Map of the upper Great Plains and Rocky Mountains region], respectfully presented to Col. D. D. Mitchell by P. J. de Smet." 1851. G4050 1851 .S6.

Pages 14–15 Powell, J. W. "Map of linguistic stocks of American Indians." 1890. G3301.E3 1890 .M3 TIL.

Page 16 Hornaday, William Temple. Map illustrating the extermination of the American bison, prepared by W. T. Hornaday; compiled under the direction of Henry Gannett, E.M. Washington: Govt. Print. Off., 1889 QI1 .U5 1887 G3301.D4. 1889. Issued with United States. National Museum. Annual report of the Board of regents of the Smithsonian institution . . . Report, 1887.

Page 17 Royce, Charles C. Indian land cessions in the United States, comp. by Charles C. Royce, with introduction by Cyrus Thomas—Colorado I. E51 .U55 18th part of Smithsonian Institution. Bureau of American Ethnology. Eighteenth annual report . . . 1896–97. Pt. 2, p. 521–997, 67 maps (part double). 30 cm.

Page 18 Vélez y Escalante, Antonio. Derrotero hecho por Antonia Vélez y Escalante, misionero para mejor conocimiento de las misiones, pueblos de indios y presidios que se hallan en el Camino de Monterrey a Santa Fe de Nuebo Mexico. 1777. G4300 1777 .V4 Vault.

Page 24 Lewis, Samuel. 1803, Louisiana Purchase, Louisiana. [S.l., 1805] From Arrowsmith & Lewis New and Elegant General Atlas, 1804. G4050 1805 .L4 TIL.

Page 25 Pike, Zebulon Montgomery. Atlas accompanying An account of expeditions to the sources of the Mississippi and through the western parts of Louisiana to the sources of the Arkansaw, Kans, La Platte, and Pierre Jaun rivers. Philadelphia, C. & A. Conrad, 1810. G1380 .P5 1810.

Pages 26–27 Long, Stephen Harriman. Country drained by the Mississippi/drawn by S.H. Long. [Philadelphia]: Young & Delleker, [1823]. G4042. M5 1823 .L6.

Pages 28–29 Frémont, John Charles. Map of an exploring expedition to the Rocky Mountains in the year 1842 and to Oregon & north California in the years 1843–44/by Brevet Capt. J. C. Frémont of the Corps of Topographical Engineers under the orders of Col. J. J. Abert, Chief of the Topographical Bureau. [Washington, D.C.?: s.n., 1845?] G4051.S12 1844 .F7 Vault: Fil 139.

Pages 30–31 Disturnell, John. Mapa de los Estados Unidos de Méjico: segun lo organizado y definido por las varias actas del congreso de dicha república y construido por las mejores autoridades. New York: J. Disturnell, 1847. G4410 1847 .D5 Vault.

Pages 32–33 Egloffstein, F. W. Skeleton map exhibiting the route explored by Capt. J. W. Gunnison U.S.A., 38 parallel of north latitude (1853), also that of the 41 parallel of latitude explored by Lieutenant E. G. P. Beckwith 3d. Arty., (1854). N[ew] Y[ork], 1855. G4051.P3 1855 .E34 RR 164.

Page 34 General geological map of Colorado Department of the Interior, U.S. Geological and Geographical Survey of the Territories; F. V. Hayden, U.S. geologist in charge. 1877.

Page 35 Hartley French Dickson & Co. Map of the recently discovered gold regions in Western Kansas & Nebraska, from actual surveys notes & observations by Hartley French Dickson & Co. [S.l.: s.n, 1859?] G4201.H2 1859 .H3.

Pages 40–41 Routes to the Pikes Peak gold regions. [S.l. : s.n., 186-] G4051.P1 186- .R6.

Pages 42–43 McGowan, D. Map of the United States west of the Mississippi showing the routes to Pike's Peak, overland mail route to California and Pacific rail road surveys. To which are added the new state & territorial boundaires[sic], the principal mail & rail road routes with all the arrangements & cor-

rections made by Congress up to the date of its issue. Compiled and drawn from U.S. land & coast surveys and other reliable sources, by D. McGowan and Geo. H. Hildt. St. Louis, Leopold Gast & Bro., 1859. G4050 1859 .M2 RR 176.

Pages 44–45 Ebert, Frederick J. Map of Colorado Territory embracing the Central Gold Region, drawn by Frederick J. Ebert; under direction of the Governor Wm. Gilpin. Philadelphia: Jacob Monk, 1862 (Philad[elphi]a: Thos. Sinclair's Lith.) G4310 1862 .E2 Vault.

Pages 46–47 Colton, J. H. Colton's rail-road and military map of the United States, Mexico, the West Indies, &c. New York, 1862. G3700 1862 .C65 RR 45.

Pages 48–49 Boyd, E. D. Map of part of the United States exhibiting the principal mail routes west of the Mississippi River. [S.l.], 1867. G4051.P8 1867 .B6 TIL.

Pages 50 and 54–55 Williams, Henry. New transcontinental map of the Pacific R.R. and routes of overland travel to Colorado, Nebraska, the Black Hills, Utah, Idaho, Nevada, Montana, California and the Pacific Coast, c. 1877. G4051.P3 1877. WSRR511.

Pages 56–57 Mota, Alb von. Map of the Denver and Rio Grande Railway and connections. [n.p., 1873]. G4321.P3 1873 .M6 RR 398.

Pages 58–59 Eccles, S. W. Map of the Denver & Rio Grande Railway, showing its connections and extensions also the relative position of Denver and Pueblo to all the principal towns and mining regions of Colorado and New Mexico. Chicago, c1881. G4311.P3 1881 .E25 RR 399.

Pages 60–61 Indexed map of Colorado showing the railroads in the state, and the express company doing business over each, also counties and rivers. Rand McNally and Company. Chicago, 1879. G4310 1879 .R3 RR 190.

Pages 62–63 The Santa Fé route Atchison, Topeka & Santa Fé R.R. 3 lines between the Missouri River and the Pacific coast to the city of Mexico via the A.T.&S. and Mexican Central R.R. Poole Brothers. Chicago, 1884. G4051.P3 1884 .P6 RR 323.

Page 64 How the public domain has been squandered, map showing the 139,403,026 acres of the people's land—equal to 871,268 farms of 160 acres each, worth at $2 an acre, $278,806,052, given by Republican Congresses to railroad corporations, Rand, McNally & Co., Engr's. Chicago, 1884. G3701.P1 1884 .R3.

Page 67 Houghton, Merritt Dana. [Fort Collins, Colorado. M. D.] Houghton. [n.p., 1865?] G4314. F4A3 1865 .H6.

Pages 68–69 Colton's new sectional map of the State of Colorado. G.W. & C.B. Colton & Co. New York: G.W. & C.B. Colton & Co., 1878. G43101878. C6.

Pages 70–71 Flett, J. H. Bird's eye view of the city of Denver, Colorado, 1881. Drawn by J. H. Flett. [n.p., 1881]. G4314.D4A3 1881 .F6.

Pages 72–73 Stoner, J. J. Bird's eye view of Greeley, Colo. county seat of Weld Co. Beck & Pauli, lithographers. Madison, Wis., c1882. G4314.G8A3 1882 .S7.

Pages 74–75 Stoner, J. J. Black Hawk, Colo. Beck & Pauli, lithographers. Madison, Wis., c1882. G4314. B32A3 1882 .S7.

Pages 76–77 Stoner, J. J. Panoramic bird's eye view of Colorado Springs, Colorado City and Manitou, Colo. 1882. Beck & Pauli, lithographers. Madison, Wis., c1882. G4314.C5A3 1882 .S7.

Pages 78–79 Houghton, Merritt Dana. [Fort Collins, Colorado] Drawn by M. D. [n.p.] 1899. G4314. F4A3 1899 .H6.

Pages 80–81 Wellge, H. (Henry). Pikes Peak panorama. Milwaukee, Wis., American Publishing Co. [1890]. G4314.C5A3 1890 .W4.

Page 82 Map of Southwestern Colorado, 1893. G4310 1893.F5.

Page 83 Kohfahl, John. "Map of great western Central City. (Imaginary place)," Robert A. Welcke, photolith., New York c1887. G9930 1887 .K6.

Page 84 Pezolt, F. (Frank). Colorado/Caxton Co.; drawn & lith. by F. Pezolt. Denver, James McConnell. 1894. G4310 1894 .C3 TIL.

Page 87 Wellge, H. (Henry). Bird's eye view of Leadville, Colo. H. Wellge, del. Beck & Pauli, lithographers. Madison, Wis., J. J. Stoner, c1882. G4314. L5A3 1882 .W4.

Pages 88–89 Stoner, J. J. Bird's eye view of Maysville, Colo. Chaffee County. Beck & Pauli, lithographers. Madison, Wis., c1882. G4314.M37A3 1882 .S7.

Pages 90–91 Stoner, J. J. Trinidad, Colo., county seat of Las Animas County. Beck & Pauli, lithographers. Madison, Wis., c1882. G4314.T7A3 1882 .S7.

Pages 92–93 Wellge, H. (Henry). Perspective map of the city of Denver, Colo. H. Wellge, des. Milwaukee, American Publishing Co. [1889]. G4314. D4A3 1889 .W4.

Pages 94–95 Pueblo, Colo. American Publishing Co. (Milwaukee, Wis.) 1890. G4314.P8A3 1890 .A6.

Pages 96–97 Koch, Augustus. Bird's eye view of Aspen, Pitkin Co., Colo. *Aspen Times* 1893. G4314. A72A3 1893 .K6.

Pages 98–99 Pezolt, F. (Frank). Colorado/Caxton Co.; drawn & lith. by F. Pezolt. Denver, James McConnell. 1894. G4310 1894 .C3 TIL.

Pages 100–101 Amerine, C. H. Cripple Creek mining district, the great gold camp of Colorado/bird's eye view by C.H. Amerine; compliments of the Cripple Creek *Sunday Herald* Souvenir ed., 1895. Cripple Creek [Colo.]: C.H. Amerine, c1895 (Denver: Denver Lith. Co.). G4314.C9A3 1895 .A4.

Pages 102–103 Cripple Creek, Phillips & Desjardins. Denver, Western Litho. Co., c1896. G4314.C9A3 1896 .P5.